MY RIDE THROUGH LIFE

A CAMBRIDGE KID FINDS IDENTITY IN DIRT LOTS, CITY SCHOOLS, AND REGGAE BEATS

ANTHONY BECKWITH

Cover design by Anthony Beckwith

Front cover photo by Daniel Beckwith

ISBN (ebook): 979-8-9931087-1-1

ISBN (paperback): 979-8-9931087-0-4

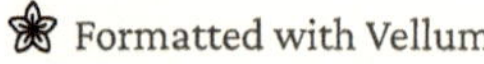
Formatted with Vellum

CONTENTS

FOREWORD

Why Write a Memoir?

I had a problem, and it was with history.

Just like my fellow students, I sat through all the years of required history courses in school. I took notes, did the readings, completed homework assignments. But for me, none of the events or people or places we studied ever seemed to come alive. I saw words on a page, but not much more; I had trouble seeing the point of it all. Despite this, I've always had a nostalgic sensibility, captivated by the sights and the sounds and the people from the past.

As a kid, watching old black-and-white movies would transport me back to an era of ice boxes, sleek steel-bodied cars, and fast-talking characters with big city accents. The film *Dead End* took me right into the New York City of the 1930s, where I imagined being one of those kids, hanging out on the front stoop of a tenement apartment, building a clubhouse in an abandoned basement, and finding clever ways to outwit the police. While eating breakfast, I would listen to old radio programs like *The Shadow* and *The Green Hornet,* the reruns airing each morning on

WBZ radio in the early 1970s, and lose myself in the suspenseful music and smooth sound of the actors' voices which conjured up images of the stories they told. I was transfixed by episodes of the hilarious 1950s TV show *The Honeymooners*, set in a gritty Brooklyn tenement building. And I was wowed by the doo-wop songs of the 1950s, with their simple but beautiful harmonies.

It wasn't until my college years that I became interested in history, even though I majored in mathematics. I dove headfirst into "alternative histories"—the ones that told more in-depth stories than the typical high school history books, weren't afraid to critique the way the American story had been told in the past, and were often written by authors outside of the mainstream. I took a course on the history of the native peoples of America, another about the Harlem Renaissance of the 1920s, and others about the history of jazz and the history of Apartheid in South Africa. I read books about the actions of the CIA in Central America, and when the latest copy of the progressive news magazine *The Nation* arrived at my dorm room, I soaked up the details about historical and current political events going on around the world. *Now* I was interested.

After getting married and starting a family, I also got bitten by the genealogy bug, wanting answers to questions like: *Where did my ancestors live? What did they do for work? What was life like for them? How and why did some of them make the journey to America? How did their experiences trickle down to affect how I've lived my life?*

In recent years, I've developed a hobby of researching not just my own family's history, but also doing deep dives into family histories for friends, co-workers, and even strangers. I've been uncovering details of how everyday people have lived their lives and how those lives were intertwined with the historical events unfolding around them. This research has helped to quench my thirst, in a deeper way than the old movies could, for a tangible connection to the past.

* * * * *

The connection I was finding between people's stories and my understanding of history strengthened as I read biographies, autobiographies, and memoirs of several well-known figures[1]. All that reading led me to a realization: that people's early lives—long before they became famous and in the public eye—could be just as fascinating as the story of their later successes. Hearing how Viola Davis or David Suzuki navigated their neighborhoods, dealt with their families, got into fights, responded to their teachers and school systems, or got their first paying jobs—all of that was just as interesting to me as learning about Davis' celebrated acting career or Suzuki's important work in science and media. To me, the narratives of their early lives could have stood on their own, even without the knowledge and details of who those young people would later become.

I came to believe two things. First, that anyone who has lived a long enough life has stories to tell that others are going to find interesting and could even give readers new perspectives on themselves, on cultures outside of their own, or on familiar historical events[2]. Second, that memoirs and autobiographies are important records. My maternal grandfather was given help to tell the story of his early life—he lived into his late 90s—but my other three grandparents don't have a written record of what their lives were like. Before I knew my older relatives as senior citizens, I know they had full and interesting lives as kids and young adults and explored and loved and made mistakes. But those stories have been lost, along with a chance to have a fuller understanding of the complexity of their personalities and identities.

---

1. These include Sidney Poitier's *This Life*, Viola Davis' *Finding Me: A Memoir*, David Suzuki's *David Suzuki: The Autobiography*, Walter Isaacson's *Ben Franklin: An American Life*, Mel Brooks' *All About Me: My Remarkable Life in Show Business,* and most recently Patti Harnigan's *August Wilson: A Life* and *Source Code* by Bill Gates.
2. Studs Terkel's books *Work* and *Division Street*, are some of the best examples of this - they are simply about "What do you do for work?," "What is your neighborhood like?," "What is your life like?," but the answers always reveal so much more.

As with most children, my sons know very little of what their father's life was like before they were born. Telling my story can fill in holes in their understanding of how I came to be the person they know today. It's also possible that decades—or even centuries—from now, historians (or anyone with an interest in history) could find themselves reading a memoir like mine—with all the adventures, triumphs, failures, and joys that are part of the everyday life of a non-public figure—and have it contribute to their understanding of a culture that may have long since faded into the past.

I believe that everyone's story is "worth telling" and that every one of those stories has the potential to have an impact on the perspective, outlook, and understanding of those who take the time to read them. I can only start by telling mine.

INTRODUCTION

Identity

I am a White male.
I was born at the end of the baby boom generation and the start of Generation X.
I am a father, a son, a brother, a husband, a cousin, a nephew, a friend.
I'm an American, with English and Jewish and Irish and German ancestors.
I'm a New Englander, a Bay Stater, a Cantabridgian, an Arlingtonian.
I'm a teacher, a coder, a genealogist, a reggae musician, a volunteer, a colleague, a reader.
I have a college education and I'm part of the American "middle class."

I am a vegetarian, a Democrat, a bicycler, a cook, a gardener, a cat lover, a music lover, an environmentalist, and a collector of things.
I'm a people-watcher, fascinated by similarities and differences and by personalities and experiences.

I believe in optimism and the power of people. I love to laugh.
I try not to jump to conclusions; I want to know more.
I've never had a sip of coffee in my life, but my sweet tooth has always gotten the better of me.

I have fears, along with insecurities and inconsistencies; I wear masks. I make mistakes.
I have ideas and I thrive on organizing and completing tasks.
Whatever it takes.

I like to problem-solve and fix things, but I can be stubborn, thinking my way is the best. At the same time, I'm in awe of what can be accomplished through honest collaboration with others.
I like to set goals and find out if they can be achieved.
I care.

But...do these things describe "me"?

Is this who I am?

What *is* the essence of a person? Is a newborn like a tree seedling, which has all of the information it needs in that tiny package to grow up to be a wise, strong, sturdy, majestic thing of the forest? Aristotle famously wrote: "Give me a child until he is seven and I will show you the man." If you think back to your seven-year-old self, you could ask this question: are you essentially the "same person" today that you were when you were seven years old? At that point, you certainly had formed your own opinions, likes and dislikes, and a personality. Are the qualities that defined you then still the ones that define who you are today—just with a few new traits sprinkled on top like a garnish? Or are you a wholly different person today than when you were small? Is that even possible?

Taking a look at this from another angle, you could ask yourself what has been your most consistent attribute or interest over your lifetime. Have you always been a painter or a writer or a musician—ever since you were young? Is there something in your life that you've almost never gone without? For me, the most consistent activity over the course of my lifetime would be bicycling. I started riding a bike around age five and have consistently spent significant time riding a bike over every one of the fifty-five years that followed.[1] I rode a bike throughout high school and in college to get to classes and continued as an adult, using a bike for transportation and for exercise and enjoyment. I rode my bike to run an errand this morning before writing this paragraph.

If you can find that thing that's the most consistent in the entirety of your life, it could be something that is connected with the unchanging essence of who you are.[2] What does such a strong and consistent life-long connection to bicycling or art or writing or singing reveal about you as a person? *Why* has that thing been so consistent in your life? Why has it been important to you to maintain it?

The question of determining your true identity is a challenging one; defining a person is an almost impossible task. One of the reasons for my decision to write an account of my life was so that I could take a ride down that road towards an answer. Maybe, for you, taking in the details of one person's life will help you to at least consider the answers to these questions for yourself—and even be inspired to sit down and begin to tell your own unique story.

---

1. I did have a few months off from biking after I fractured my tibia in 2014, in the only bike accident I've ever had.
2. If you look back and can't find interests or activities that have remained consistent throughout your life, maybe the constant for you is, instead, a set of values or beliefs.

Author's Note

In this memoir, I refer to my parents as "Barbara" and "Jon" and not as "mom" and "dad" or some other form of those words. This is not something I've done simply for the reader—it's what I have always called my parents.

My parents have been social activists most of their adult lives and have held many counter-cultural beliefs over the years, including a general rejection of obedience to authority figures whose claim to authority is simply based on their position or their moniker: teacher, coach, police officer, politician, parent. Calling someone "coach," "sir," "officer," "Mr." or "Dr." was something they rejected in the same way that many people during this same period began to object to the use of "Mrs."/"Miss" and replace them with "Ms."

As a result, I was raised to call my parents by their first names and have done so for my entire life, other than briefly at about age twelve.[3] While it may seem awkward to people when they hear it for the first time, it's who we are as a family, and it gives our family a uniqueness that I now embrace.

• **Other Names:** This memoir is a work of nonfiction, and so I've included the names of real people and real places, and I'm describing real events. When I refer to family members and ancestors and public figures, I sometimes use both their first and last names. For most non-family members who are non-public figures, I've included *only their first name.* If a situation is particularly sensitive for a specific individual, I've used a fictitious name and have used quotation marks around the name the first time it is referenced.

---

3. Being self-conscious at that age and not wanting to stand out, I tried to switch over to calling them "Mom" and "Dad" but it just didn't stick, and I eventually got over my reluctance.

• **Memory:** I have used my own recollections, past writings, research, and help from family and friends to be able to describe actual events, as they occurred, as accurately as possible. But individual memories and even collective memories can become clouded and questionable over time. I've done my best to ensure that my descriptions are true to the events as they occurred. If I have not achieved perfection in this area, please forgive me.

• **Black and White:** When referring to what we call "race" in America, "black" and "white" are very commonly used terms. In writing this book, I spent some time delving into the ongoing debates about whether or not to apply capitalization to one of these terms, the other, or to both. There's no single authority on this issue. I've decided that when I am using those two terms in reference to people, or groups of people, I will capitalize each. I do this to differentiate those cultural racial words from the lowercase versions of the words, which in my mind refer only to the two extreme colors (colors that are not the skin tones of actual people). I also think this aligns those terms with others like "Hispanic" and "Native American," which are always capitalized.

PART I: GROWING

1

FAMILY ROOTS

IN 1935, FRANKLIN DELANO ROOSEVELT was serving in his second year as president and was struggling to deal with the effects of the Great Depression and an unemployment rate hovering around twenty percent. James Michael Curley was in his first year serving as the governor of Massachusetts, after serving three terms as the City of Boston's mayor (in the coming years, he would be imprisoned for mail fraud, the least of his crimes). On Christmas Day of that year, the hit film *Little Women*, starring Katherine Hepburn, played at the University Theatre in Cambridge, as gentle snow began to fall in the Boston area.[1]

Just a mile or so up the street from the theater, on that same evening of December 25, 1935, a young Mildred Beckwith found herself inside a birthing room in one of the old brick buildings at the *Cambridge Hospital* on Mt. Auburn Street (a decade later it would be renamed *Mt. Auburn Hospital*). Mildred's husband Manny was down the hall, nervously awaiting news of the birth of the couple's first child. He needn't have worried: Mildred gave

1. The front page of that morning's *Boston Globe* predicted the weather for the day to be "Generally fair, snow flurries and colder at night." What actually fell out of the sky later that evening is harder to determine.

birth to a healthy baby boy that evening—a boy who would eventually grow up to become my father, *Jonathan Roger Beckwith,* going by the name *Jonny* as a kid, then by *Jon* after he grew wings and flew.

Two days later, little Jonny was wrapped up to stay warm and gently carried in Manny's arms as he and Mildred walked their baby home to their rental apartment at 15 Longfellow Road, directly across the street from the hospital.

Boston: My Father's Family

What do any of us know about our parents' past lives? We essentially "get to know them" only after they are fully formed, having already passed through childhood and adolescence, finished all their schooling, and found their way into adulthood. To a child, it's as if your parents were born at the same moment that you were—but unlike you, your parents were born big and strong and experienced enough to raise you and provide for you. The story of your parents, and their parents in turn, is essential (for better or worse) to understanding who you are and who you have become.

MY GRANDFATHER *Manuel Beckwith*[2] was born and then grew up in the Boston neighborhood of Dorchester, near Blue Hill Avenue, which was a major thoroughfare adjacent to Franklin Park. Franklin Park is the largest link in what is still called "the Emerald Necklace," an urban green space planned by Frederick Law Olmsted in the 1880s to help provide an escape from the busy and dirty city. As a teenager in the late 1920s, Manny surely must have spent time wandering the rolling paths of that park, the sounds of

2. Manny was born in 1911 as Manuel *Berkowitz*, but changed his name at age 21 to Beckwith, as did several of his relatives. His name-change application cited people's difficulty pronouncing his name, but more likely the reason was anti-Jewish discrimination in employment.

birds mingling with the roaring of early automobiles and with the noise coming out of the shops up and down the busy avenue.[3]

Manny's parents, *Jacob "JB" Berkowitz*[4] and *Sarah Sodekson*, had met and married while living in the old and crowded West End neighborhood of Boston, moving to Dorchester in 1909. Manny was born two years later into a tight-knit neighborhood that included many of his aunts, uncles, and cousins, having all made the same move from the West End at around the same time.

Jon's mother *Sylvia Mildred Rosenberg*, who went by *Mildred* starting at an early age, also grew up in Dorchester, making both Manny and Mildred "city kids" by nature. By the time she was fourteen, her family had moved from Dorchester to the Allston neighborhood of Boston, not far from the Boston University campus. Mildred attended the Girls Latin School in Boston, which at the time was near Huntington Avenue, not far from the Harvard Medical School. The circumstances of their meeting has been lost to history, but by the time they had reached their early twenties, Manny and Mildred had hatched a plan to be married—they eloped to New York City in 1933, immediately returning to Boston to start their new lives together.

Mildred's mother was *Jennie Lewis* (born *Jennie Lecznisky* in Lithuania), a school teacher and amateur actress. Mildred's father, *Isaac Rosenberg*, whose father had emigrated from Poland, was raised in Portland, Maine. After Isaac and Jennie's marriage–and before Mildred was born—they moved from Portland to Dorchester. Isaac had recently become a practicing dentist, and he found office space in old Scollay Square, known as a popular and busy section of Boston with several theaters and a wide variety of shops.[5]

---

3. Manny attended Dorchester High School and at one point was punished for leading a protest against compulsory military drill at the school.

4. Jacob's family name in Lithuania was Zif, but it was changed to Berkowitz upon arrival in Boston.

5. It was in the 1940s that Scollay Square began to deteriorate and the old grand theaters began to cater to sailors, hosting mostly burlesque shows. The entire area

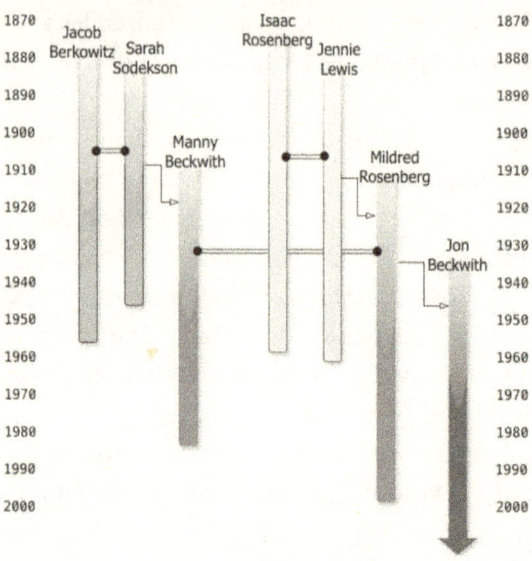

My father's side of the family—the people described above—were all descendants of Eastern European Jews who fled persecution in their homelands. The first were the Rosenbergs in the 1870s, followed by the Sodeksons, the Berkowitzes, and the Leczniskys, all in the 1890s. It was a period of time when Jews in Eastern Europe were forced to live and work in restricted areas (the so-called "Pale of Settlement"), faced the threat of random violence from mobs ("pogroms") worked up by government-backed antisemitic laws and propaganda, and could only watch helplessly as their children were conscripted into the Russian army for brutal 25-year terms. The majority of Jews in Lithuania and Poland lived in poor conditions with little ability to rise above them, and so making the long journey to America—and for most of my father's ancestors, the Boston area—represented an escape to a place where they could experience freedom of movement, freedom of worship, and opportunities for prosperity. Of course,

---

was razed in 1962 and much of Boston City Hall now sits upon the ghosts of Scollay. Isaac's office was on Hanover Street and by 1938 was at 6 Scollay Square.

when they arrived here after having made the long journey by boat, they had no way of knowing if their "American Dream" would indeed become a reality.

* * * * *

AFTER THEIR WEDDING, Manny and Mildred eventually moved to an apartment in Cambridge, Massachusetts. At the time my father was born, Mildred had just graduated from Radcliffe College, a feat made financially possible by her father Issac's resolve and hard work to become a practicing dentist (Isaac's father Simon didn't have much, if any, formal education and was a peddler and later ran a small clothing shop in Portland, Maine). Mildred would later get her master's degree in education and become a classroom teacher.

My grandfather Manny was working for his father's business, *Hub Cycle & Auto Supply* (originally just *Hub Cycle*), which at the time was in the Haymarket area of Boston. His father JB first established the *Hub Cycle* bicycle shop in Boston's North End in 1897, just two years after he arrived in America at age sixteen with little money and no English.[6] Despite having minimal formal education and no formal business training, JB's shop had by the 1920s grown into a successful business and moved to a larger building. They sold bicycle, motorcycle, and auto parts, along with radios and a variety of other products. Manny started attending Boston University in 1928, but during the Great Depression he decided to withdraw in order to help his father keep his bicycle business afloat.

Manny and Mildred appreciated life in Cambridge, with Manny commuting to work in Boston and the two of them getting to know their neighbors and spending time with their infant son. But they were searching for a place where they could buy their

---

6. JB had begun apprenticing as a blacksmith in his early teens in Lithuania, so bicycle-building was a natural fit for him.

own home to raise their new and growing family. By 1939, five years after moving to Cambridge, they found a home in the Auburndale section of Newton, Massachusetts, on a quiet inlet of the Charles River. They were the only Jewish family in their neighborhood, but the Beckwith family would quickly become good friends with some of their Italian-American neighbors and were soon an integral part of the community.

Manny and Mildred had two more children over the next five years (Gail and Pepi), all three of them attending the well-respected Newton Public Schools. In the winter, the kids ice-skated on the river, tracing long figure-eights until the sun went down. In the summertime, they would visit (or sometimes sneak into) the famed Norumbega Park around the corner, as well as spending time exploring the wilderness around the banks of the Charles.

After graduating from Newton North High School in 1953, Jon returned to the city of his birth—this time to attend college. In the fall, he started at Harvard University in Cambridge as a mathematics major. Harvard had set restrictive quotas starting in the 1920s, capping the number of Jews, Blacks, and Catholics that could be admitted[7]. This discriminatory policy continued until the 1960s, but Jon was apparently lucky enough that his application made it through under the quota, allowing it to be considered on its merit. In Jon's time at Harvard, he made great friends and would spend time talking deep into the night with his fellow students about literature and jazz and the politics of the times. (He would eventually become disillusioned by the abstractness of mathematics and switch his major to chemistry, a change which eventually led to his finding his passion in the field of genetics.)

New York: My Mother's Family

---

7. Harvard went so far as to classify students as "J1," "J2" or "J3" for "conclusively Jewish," "probably Jewish" or "maybe Jewish," according to a 2022 Supreme Court amicus brief.

BARBARA'S MOTHER (my grandmother), *Marian Lucinda Hunter,* was born and raised in Brooklyn, New York. Her mostly Protestant ancestors had been in the greater New York City area for many generations. At least one of them fought for independence in the American Revolution and another in a New York State regiment in the Civil War. One of her ancestors had even come over on the Mayflower.

Marian's mother, *Mary Fletcher Stokehill,* had crossed the ocean with her family in a steamship as a little girl, landing in New York City in 1889 and settling in Brooklyn. She'd left the British port city of Leeds with her carpenter father, who expected to get work building benches for American trolleys and trains—work which was soon replaced by machines, leaving him unemployed. Mary worked for a time in a sweatshop in Brooklyn, making ties.

Marian's father, *William T. Hunter Jr.*, worked his way up to an executive position at the Schrader Valve Company in Brooklyn.[8] This success was important for William because his father had been injured serving in the Union Army in the Civil War but refused to take a government pension, which left the family with little money. Williams's position at Schrader Valve eventually gave him the means to amply provide for his children, allowing for creature comforts like a summer place in the Pennsylvania woods, tuition for college educations, and foreign travel. His daughter Marian—my grandmother—attended Wellesley College in Massachusetts, majoring in social work.

Barbara's father, *Joseph Theodore Shutt*[9] was born and raised in small-town, working-class Boalsburg, Pennsylvania, surrounded by rolling mountains, deep woods, and fast-moving rivers.

---

8. Schrader valves were mostly used for bicycle tubes at the time—automobiles had not yet caught on—and this was around the same time that my father's grandfather JB was working in the bicycle business in Boston. Since those bicycles surely used Schrader valves, there's a possibility that these two companies did some kind of business with each other.

9. Joseph Theodore Shutt was actually born Joseph *William* Shutt.

Joe's mother, *Ausie Marie Johnston*, was from Pleasant Gap, Pennsylvania. She may have been a beekeeper, but we do know that her father had been a day laborer.

Joe's father, *Walker Stine Shutt*, started out as a laborer and worked his way up to a position as a concrete contractor. He ran crews for various projects, building roads and working on bridges in and around Pennsylvania. His father before him had been a laborer and farmer.

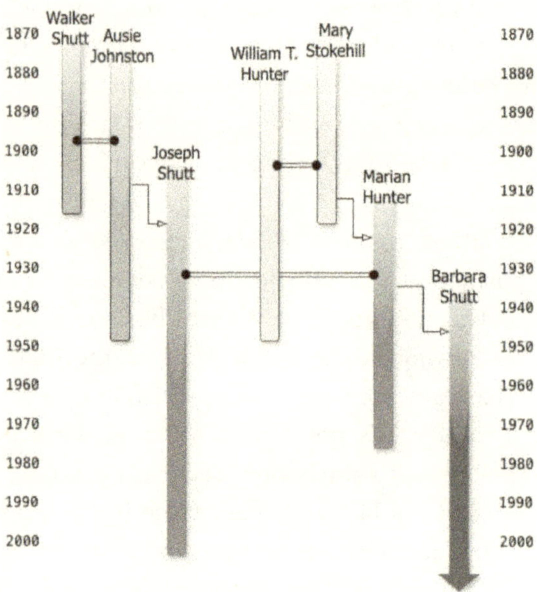

Joe Shutt

The Shutt name is thought by our family to have Germanic roots (likely originating as *Schutt*), but no one knows for sure. Germans certainly were early settlers of the region of Pennsylvania where the Shutts made their home. German tradesmen and artisans began arriving there after fleeing both religious persecution and the devastation of the Thirty Years War in Europe in the mid-1600s.

Tragically, my "grampa Joe" was only eleven years old when his father, Walker, died in a horrific train accident while working on the William Penn Highway, adjacent to the train tracks. This devastated young Joe, and it forced him to go to work quite early in life. He trapped skunks and possums and sold their pelts to help pay for food. Later he trimmed pine trees to help in the work of combatting the boll weevil infestation of 1917. He also did farm work, milking cows and driving ploughs with horses. He worked in a silk mill. He dug ditches for an electric company. He helped to build roads and trails and telephone poles for the Forestry Department. He worked as a plumber's helper. All of this was before he was nineteen years old.

Joe later attended Franklin & Marshall College (F&M) on an athletic scholarship. Attending F&M fundamentally altered how he viewed himself and who he could become. He felt he was hashing out "the problems of the world" with his professors and they made him feel like he could make a real difference. Joe majored in economics, made many friends, and became well-known as a football player, a track star, and a champion wrestler (he was the captain of all three teams).

Upon graduating in 1930, he moved to New York City to work for the New York Telephone Company, which had recruited him and other friends from F&M. For a time, he lived at the Central Branch of the YMCA in Manhattan, but later got an apartment with a man named David Hunter in Brooklyn. David Hunter, as it turns out, had a sister: Marian Hunter. That connection led to "Joe from Pennsylvania" meeting "Marian from Brooklyn" and to their ensuing courtship. Marian and Joe were married in 1933 and moved in to an apartment on East 21st Street in the Midwood section of Brooklyn.

* * * * *

EARLY IN THE FALL OF 1937, Marian Lucinda Hunter Shutt gave birth to my mother, *Barbara Shutt,* in Brooklyn. My mother was the middle child—Linda had come before her and Joanne would come after.

Shortly after my mother was born, the family was on the move—at first to Bellrose, Long Island; then to Garden City, Long Island; and later to Chatham, New Jersey, where Barbara attended high school. She played flute in the band and was a prolific writer, working on newsletters and writing the end-of-year blurbs about the students for the yearbook. In 1955, upon graduation from high school, Barbara left the New York area and headed to New England, where she attended Wellesley College as an English major, continuing her passion for the written word.

Barbara Shutt had chosen Wellesley over Bennington and Middlebury, both colleges in rural Vermont towns. On her visit to Wellesley, she had fallen in love with the beautiful campus and with its serene lake at the bottom of the hill. It also had the advantage of being not far from two vibrant cities—Boston and Cambridge.

Jon Beckwith had chosen Harvard over other area colleges (like Brown University in Rhode Island), opting instead for the familiar surroundings of Cambridge and the excellent reputation of Harvard.

In an alternate universe where either of them had chosen differently, the words you are reading on this page would dissolve before your eyes.

Manny Beckwith, Mildred Rosenberg, Marian Hunter, Joe Shutt

2

YOU DON'T HAVE TO DANCE WITH THE ONE THAT BRUNG YA

IF YOU'VE GOT a "good arm," you could throw a small rock from the intersection of Memorial Drive and today's JFK Street, over the riverbank on the Cambridge side, and right into the Charles River. In 1931, on that same corner, Harvard finally completed their multi-year project of building a new four-story brick dormitory (at the time, JFK Street was still known as Boylston Street).[1] The dorm was named *Eliot House* after the previous president of Harvard, Charles Eliot, who had served as its leader for an astonishing forty years (no other president before, or since, has ever served more than 24 years).

It appears that Eliot deserved to have *something* named after him because among his many contributions were the building of the massive Harvard Stadium—where, in 1979, Bob Marley would play in front of a packed house, and where Harvard football home games have been played for close to a hundred years—as well as the introduction of electives at Harvard, which likely elicited a campus-wide sigh of relief from the undergrads. This Eliot House

1. The area had been marshland in the past, but had housed a power station in the years right before the dorm was built.

dormitory would play an important role—just for a moment—in how I came to be.

One night, in late January of 1957, a young Harvard student named Roger had a lot going on. Not only was he throwing a party at his dorm in Eliot House, but he had a date for the night—and she needed a ride.

Nineteen-year-old Barbara Shutt had likely been working hard on her second semester classes at Wellesley all week and would have been ready to step away from her studies and find *some* kind of distraction. Fortunately, she had an invitation to a party. Her date for that night would be a man named Roger. Barbara knew that he was a sophomore at Harvard and had an interest in English and drama, but not much more.

That night, Roger made the long drive out to Wellesley College to pick Barbara up from 210 Tower Court East, her room in the Gothic-style dormitory she had been assigned to. The car ride back to Cambridge must have taken a while, given that the faster route along the Massachusetts Turnpike wouldn't open to the public until later that year. The young couple eventually arrived back at Eliot House to find the party in full swing.

Meanwhile, twenty-one-year-old Jon Beckwith had left his boarding room at 25 Carver Street[2], a bit west of Harvard Square, and was walking down Massachusetts Avenue in the cold, making his way towards Harvard Square. He was on his way to the same Eliot House party.

JON AND BARBARA likely didn't even notice each other at the

---

2. At the time, in a letter, Jon described the Carver St. apartment this way: "The rooms are flung off one hallway like toes off a foot. The house was built with only utility in mind. My room was about wide enough and long enough for a bed and a half. Bob lived in the next room next door; he insisted upon humming all night to his music, somehow hoping that by questioning the music it might answer him."

start of the night, but a fateful pronouncement would change that. Barbara recalls that "it was announced that they were going to show a 'blue' movie in another room. I was embarrassed by this, so I told Roger that I would wait while he went to watch the movie." While Barbara sat in the main room, chin on hand, waiting for the awkwardness to pass, Jon approached her and began talking to her, assuming she had either also arrived solo or had been jilted by her date. They hit it off and ended up discussing British author Colin Wilson's philosophical book *The Outsider,* which got them talking about existentialism and alienation. They followed up with discussions about music and other topics that they were pleased to find they had a common interest in. The next day, Jon called to ask Barbara on a date to attend a performance of Samuel Beckett's *Waiting for Godot.* Roger had been long forgotten at this point.

In the coming weeks and months, Jon invited Barbara to the theater and to jazz shows and parties. Jon was smitten with Barbara's frankness, curiosity, and knowledge of poetry. Barbara was impressed by Jon's musical knowledge, singing ability, and his wide-ranging cultural and political awareness. They were both happy to find someone they were comfortable and shared interests with and were physically attracted to.

In the spring of 1957, Jon graduated from Harvard and then spent his summer biking solo through Europe, eventually meeting up with Barbara in Italy. She was living with an Italian family for the summer before returning to Wellesley for her last two years of college. Over the next year, Barbara and Jon realized that they were in love. In the fall of 1960, these two young people with such different family backgrounds became engaged to be married.

Barbara Shutt and Jonathan Beckwith were married on December 26, 1960, in Henryville, Pennsylvania, where Barbara's grandfather had established a summer home a few decades earlier and where several of her relatives now lived. Jon had just accepted a post-doctoral research fellowship at the University of

California at Berkeley, and Barbara had finished her master's of education degree at Tufts and was going to teach junior high school English in Berkeley.

Science on the Move

YOUNG JON BECKWITH was now deeply involved in the scientific community and was being exposed to exciting, creative, and innovative ideas in genetics. He became particularly inspired by a trio of microbiologists who had made major discoveries in the field. He found himself obsessed with the idea of working with them in Paris at the *Pasteur Institute.* As a result, my parents ended up moving often over the next five years, some of those moves being done with one or two sons in tow. Starting in Cambridge, Massachusetts, they moved "out west" to Berkeley, California; then "back east" to Princeton, New Jersey; then even further east, all the way to England; and eventually to Paris, France. My brother *Benjamin Hunter Beckwith* was born while they were in Princeton, on the day before Christmas, 1961.

In December of 1963, Jon, Barbara, and two-year-old Ben moved from their current apartment in London into a house for rent at 56 Glisson Road in Cambridge, England, about a half a mile walk from the centuries-old campus of Cambridge University.[3] At the time of this move, Barbara was two months pregnant with her second son.

On July 6, 1964, Barbara gave birth to *Alexander Rhys Beckwith* in Cambridge, England (because her first birth had no complications, her second birth took place in a "nursing home," rather than a hospital). The genesis of that name is a bit complicated. My parents had planned to name me *Anthony*, but after giving

3. At around age 28, I tried to make a sojourn to the 56 Glisson Road home where my parents first took me for strolls as an infant. I made it all the way to Cambridge, England, and took photos of everything. Upon returning home, I realized I had been looking at #55 the whole time, instead of #56. I was on the wrong side of the street!

birth to me, my mother thought I didn't "look like an Anthony" and so they decided on *Alexander*. When I was less than three months old, however, they decided that *Alexander* felt too much like *Benjamin*, both being multisyllabic, and they didn't like the nickname "Alex" for Alexander. Having finally made their decision, they had to fill out the British paperwork for a new birth certificate, so that my name could be changed to *Anthony Rhys Beckwith*.[4]

From Cambridge, the family moved to Paris as my father continued his scientific pursuits. My parents found an apartment in Vanves, just outside the city, and we lived there for almost a year, with my brother attending a local Montessori school. As an infant, of course, I missed out on mid-1960s Paris and all that it had to offer: the cafés, the jazz, the art, the nightlife. While living in Paris and raising two children, my parents did find the time and the inspiration to join one of the early marches against the Vietnam War, which would rage for another ten years. This would be just one of many social justice actions that they would undertake over the next several decades.

*****

IN 1965, WE RETURNED TO CAMBRIDGE, Massachusetts, where Barbara and Jon found an apartment to rent at 992 Memorial Drive, a few blocks from Mt. Auburn Hospital in one direction and from Harvard Square in the other. The building was a set of six-story brick apartments opposite the Charles River, built around 1920. We lived there for a couple of years, getting to know other apartment-dwellers and playing in the courtyard and on the cement animals in the park down the street.

At the time, my father was an Assistant Professor of Bacteriology and Immunology at Harvard Medical School and my mother was taking care of me and my brother while working

4. Rhys is a fairly popular Welsh name, meaning, "passion" or "enthusiasm."

part-time in nearby Belmont correcting English papers at the high school (she would land her first teaching job in the Boston area in 1969). In early 1967, my parents heard from their babysitting pool about an available downstairs apartment in a two-family home a few blocks away on Appleton Road and they decided it was a good move. After renting the apartment for over a year, in December of 1968, my parents signed the papers to purchase the two-family home that they had been renting. This is the home where my brother and I grew up and where my parents remained for more than six decades.

Jon Beckwith, with 25 Carver Street behind him, on the right

Barbara Beckwith, 1955 at Wellesley College

3

THOSE OLD CREAKY FLOORS

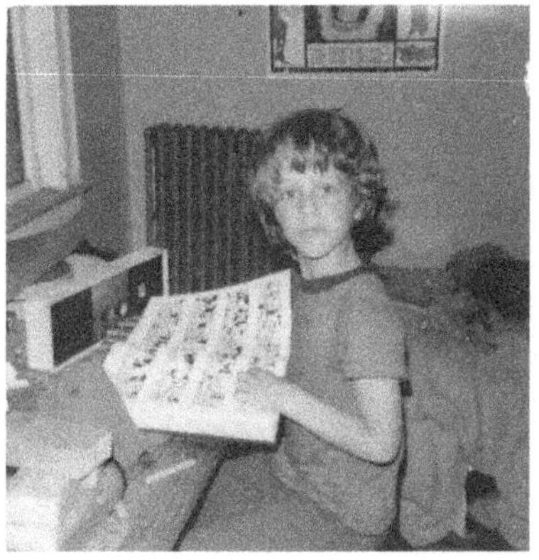

The author, circa 1975

CONSIDER A BLANK CANVAS, stretched tight on its frame. If you were to paint, on that canvas, a scene that somehow represented your childhood, what people, objects, and events would you choose to depict? What combination of colors would you need? How fine a brush would you need to render those small, almost forgotten, details of your life?

. . .

IT WAS 1971, and boy, was I ready for first grade. We had just returned to Cambridge after spending six months in Naples, Italy, where our family lived while my father was "doing science." Having already survived the rigors of kindergarten, I proudly started first grade at the Russell Elementary School, one of the twelve K-8 schools that Cambridge's population was large enough to support at the time. The Russell was an old brick building with a blacktop playground about a block from Fresh Pond.

Some of the earliest memories I have of my life are from this school. I remember the creaky wooden floors, the stairwells with large wooden banisters that gave you splinters if you weren't careful, the smell of the long line of urinals in the boys' bathroom, the steam pipes in the hallways and the humidity they'd generate in the winter, and the classrooms with large radiators and even larger windows. The school felt imposing and the teachers old-fashioned, but I made great friends there and it was only about six blocks from our house—an easy walk.

The school was built in 1897, when bicycles were king and before automobiles became popular. By the time I was in second grade and just getting started in my life, the aged and tired Russell building had reached the end of its own. I have clear memories of packing all of our supplies from the classroom into brown paper shopping bags and then following our teacher, marching the three or four blocks down the hill to the recently-completed *John M. Tobin School*, located near the intersection of Concord Avenue and Fresh Pond Parkway.[1]

Many people later said that the new Tobin School "looked like a prison" from the outside, but the inside to us felt very modern-looking—very "1972." The halls were carpeted in rich blues and reds and purples and greens, with huge carpeted circular benches under gaping circular skylights at the ends of the halls. The cafe-

1. The school was built on the site of an empty lot that before that had been a swimming hole and before that an old brickyard.

teria had two-story tall windows and modern-looking circular seats that would swing out from the modular tables. Entering through the front doors revealed a sweeping ramp that led up to the main hallway and the principal's office, and a hallway balcony overlooking the cafeteria; another ramp led down to the lower floors with classrooms for Art, Home Economics, and Woodworking. There were patios right outside most classrooms for playing ball games. The building and grounds felt very angular and geometrical, in stark contrast to the old-fashioned brick buildings we were used to.[2]

WHAT WAS IT LIKE attending the public schools in Cambridge? My experiences from kindergarten through high school in the public schools remained consistent in at least one aspect: exposure to the intricate and complex mix of cultures, ethnicities, and socioeconomic backgrounds of the Cambridge student population.

In elementary school, I met and became friends with students whose parents had moved to the Boston area from Puerto Rico or Portugal or Jamaica, and others whose families were Italian-American or Irish-American or African-American or Jewish or Anglo-Saxon. There were kids whose parents had lucrative jobs and high levels of education and others who worked in the trades or service industries—and others still that struggled just to make ends meet. In the first and second grades, I was good friends with a kid from a wealthy family who had a maid with one of those classic maid outfits you saw on television—he lived in quite a large single-family home. But I was also friends with a kid whose father was a bus driver for the MBTA and who lived in affordable housing near the city dump.

There was a lot to learn about navigating these different

2. In 2022, the Tobin School was completely demolished to make way for a new school, which had its opening just as I was finishing this book, in August of 2025.

cultures. In my mind, I saw the descendants of Italian and Irish immigrants as pretty outgoing: they were demonstrative, fun, and could entertain with their sense of humor, but were often tough kids. I was friends with some of these kids and tried to steer clear of others. I thought some of the African-American kids had cool-sounding names (like Parcella, Chantelle, Loretta and Charita, four girls that moved up through the grades with me) and by the later grades noticed that I seemed to like the same kind of music that many of them did (at the time, this was funk bands like *The Fatback Band*, *Cameo*, *The Bar-Kays*, and *Parliament*. Funk was the rich, raw, urban music of the mid-1970s which predated disco). There were sometimes conflicts between White and Black kids, but mostly kids just found things they had in common with others, regardless of background, and the friendships that developed were varied and strong.

School life for me and all of my classmates in Cambridge was a mix of learning, fun, working, and playing, but it also involved navigating the interactions between different cultures and dealing with and responding to complex events like theft, arguments, and fights. Each "day in the life" provided some new lesson to learn about humanity and was sometimes difficult, but never boring—and this was even more true when we went to high school and experienced the blending of kids from all different parts of the city.

As I got older, moving up through the Cambridge Public School system, I realized how powerful and valuable it was to be spending so much time with kids with such a diversity of experiences. The richness of cultures, the range of views on life and work: these would help me to understand, enjoy, and be empathetic to all kinds of people throughout my life.

* * * * *

I HAVE FOND MEMORIES of all the friends that came into and out of my life as we drifted through elementary school. I was very close to Bobby in first or second grade, walking up and over the hill on Appleton Street almost every day to hang out with him after school. We would watch shows like *The Three Stooges* and he always had the latest games like *Rock 'Em Sock 'Em Robots*, *Kerplip-Kerplop* and *Mouse Trap*. My friendship with Bobby is the earliest one I can remember.

I was good friends around the second and third grade with Hagop, whose father was the custodian of the Armenian church on the corner of Sparks and Brattle Streets. When it was time for his father to sweep and clean the large hall, the church pews were moved to the edges and we would get a couple of hockey sticks and play street hockey on the huge wide-open wooden floor. I remember climbing up the outdoor stairs over a low part of the roof of the church up to his family's small apartment. As I entered, I could see and smell food that was very new to me. I was never good at eating interesting foods when I was a kid, so I hope I didn't insult the family back then by refusing to eat the food from their culture—food which I would likely be impressed by today.

Around fourth or fifth grade, Mark was one of my best friends and I always looked forward to hanging out with him. He lived on Mount Auburn Street and when I visited, we would often head out on our bikes for a ride through his hilly neighborhood or stay inside and play board games or try out the boxing gloves he owned. I vividly remember listening to Stevie Wonder's *Songs in the Key of Life* for the very first time in Mark's house on their turntable in the living room—one of the greatest albums ever recorded. I looked up to Mark—he seemed smart and self-confident to me.

The story of how I met Paul is interesting. It was September of 1976, the very first day of sixth grade, and I couldn't find the classroom—not a good start to the year! By the time I did find it, I was late for class. I swung open the door to my new classroom, interrupting the teacher, and looked around at all the kids at their desks staring back at me. The problem was, I couldn't see any free place to sit—*what should I do?* I was pretty shy back then and probably had a scared look on my face. But then some kid raised his arm and waved his hand at me, offering me the open seat next to him. That was Paul, and we eventually became best friends.

Paul and I would ride our bikes, play poker with other kids, listen to music, and just generally hang out. Paul lived in Boston at the time, but the Boston Public Schools were in turmoil in the 1970s (the school busing/desegregation program created serious conflict that attracted nationwide attention), so Paul's solution was to use his friend Michael's Cambridge address and phone number to be able to attend the much calmer Cambridge Public Schools. When he couldn't stay over at a friend's house, he had a very long commute by the MBTA to go back and forth between Boston and Cambridge. Paul and I got ten-speed bikes at around the same time—mine a Raleigh, his a Free Spirit. When it was getting late at night, we would both ride our bikes to Harvard Square so he could take the subway home. I would then ride home in the dark with my left hand on my handlebars and my right hand on his bike's handlebars, guiding his riderless bike down the streets of Cambridge. For a while, Paul and I did everything together.

In sixth grade, Laurie and Eileen were best friends. Laurie had light blonde hair and sharp features. Eileen had black hair and a cute, round Irish-looking face—and freckles! I had a crush on Eileen, but I had no idea how to talk to her. I was good at talking to girls when I didn't have a crush on them, but I had no formula for what to do when I had feelings for them. At some point in sixth grade, I remember biking into Harvard Square and going to a phone booth near the old *Paperback Booksmith*, putting my dime into the slot, and dialing the phone number for Eileen's house, which I had found in the phonebook. Actually, I probably went through this ritual a few times, but each time chickened out at the last second. Finally I let the phone ring and didn't panic. But I didn't have any kind of plan for what I was going to say. So when

Eileen picked up and answered the phone, I paused, and then just blurted out "I like you!" and hung up the phone. The fact that I still remember that debacle now reflects the level of embarrassment and ineptitude I felt at my first real attempt at going out with a girl.

Paul somehow got the courage up and asked Eileen's friend Laurie out. I was in awe. They eventually became boyfriend and girlfriend for a while. My failure in sixth grade was a sign of things to come—through high school and into the start of college, I struggled with how to talk to girls, although I did stumble into a few dates and a few relationships along the way.

I don't remember my teachers quite as well as I do my friends, but I do have lasting memories of several of them. Mrs. Houston was my favorite. She was my fourth-grade teacher; probably in her early thirties, African-American, and she was wise, fun, and stylish. She also really encouraged my work in mathematics, which eventually became my college major. She even helped me out at one point when I had a kid picking on me. Jerry, for some reason, liked to tease me; he thought that he could push me around and that I wouldn't fight back. And I didn't! So one day, Mrs. Houston took me aside and said—to my surprise—"The next time he picks on you, just pick up a chair and throw it at him." Or maybe she said "threaten" to throw it at him. I remember thinking at the time that this was insane advice. *What kind of kid was I to pick up a chair in a classroom at school and threaten someone?*

A few days later, Jerry was picking on me, and what did I do but lift up a chair over my head and aim it at him, telling him to stop! He was about as shocked as I was and stopped in his tracks. That pretty much put a stop to him bothering me. The funny thing was that, in my mind, I was sure I had done this instinctively and not because of Mrs. Houston's advice to me, even though the point she made about sticking up for myself had obviously lodged itself in my head and led to my actions.

There were a few other teachers that I recall. Mr. Balf was

built like a football player and was strict, but funny. Mr. Driscoll was, sadly, best known as the teacher with the bad breath—but he seemed like a nice guy. Ms. Paddock and Ms. Stout teamed up and took an alternate approach to fifth grade education—some sort of progressive experimental thing, but I don't recall the details. Mrs. Anagnostopoulos taught us music and singing, but was met with a lot of unruly kids in her classroom. My friend Michel's mother taught French at our school (the family was from France). I always wondered what it would be like to have your mother working at the school you went to, given how much school felt like an entirely different world from the one at home.

OF COURSE, there are more stories that could be told: the time a line drive hit me right in my eye on the Tobin baseball field; the time everyone said Joe's "head got split open" (we took it literally); the poker games we played on the back steps of Tobin at night; doing "KP duty" in the Tobin kitchen; playing stickball games on the blacktop; being the scorekeeper for the basketball team; going to school fairs, lighting firecrackers, seeing kids being chased down the hall—the everyday chaos of a K-8 city school in all its glory. The main mission of a public school is to teach lessons on various academic subjects and to give students foundational skills. But it's the interactions with friends, with kids you don't know, with teachers, and with the environment, that add up to a different kind of learning.

The teachers did what they could to prepare us for high school and our adult lives, and we did what we could to make it through that developmental stage, trying to make friends and trying to have fun. Simultaneously, like a horse pulling a barge along a canal, there was a parallel childhood experience happening outside of school, which had a life all of its own.

Russell Elementary School, c.1940

Tobin School in 1972

Tobin 8th grade graduation photo. I am at the top left—the only kid whose face is partially hidden!

4

KID LIFE

The Nature of a Neighborhood

APPLETON STREET IN CAMBRIDGE starts at the bottom of a hill on Brattle Street, just a block or so from where the slow-moving Charles River widens as it winds its way to Boston. As Appleton heads northwest, it rises up, past the aptly-named Highland Avenue and then to the hill's peak. In this section of the street, the houses seem to be lording over all passersby, having been built long ago clearly by and for wealthy Cambridge families, with impressively large yards and gardens. As the street slopes down on the other side of the hill towards Huron Ave, eventually ending at Concord Ave, the housing stock transforms quickly into modest, closely-spaced two-family homes, places that were populated largely by Irish-American families in the 1940s and 1950s.[1]

Appleton *Road* is a dead-end street that branches off of

1. According to U.S. Census data I found from those decades showing family names of people living in those homes.

Appleton Street about halfway down that more crowded side of the hill. This short street is where I grew up.[2] There are only four homes with addresses on Appleton Road (all were two-family homes, although one was later converted to a single family), and our house was the only one on the street without a driveway or a garage—and still is to this day.

An important aspect of anyone's life, wherever we may live in the world, is how we interact with our neighbors. Maybe you live in a rural area and have no nearby neighbors; maybe you live in an apartment building with hundreds of neighbors. These neighbors are usually not your family and are likely not friends or colleagues, and yet you see them on a very regular basis—and in many cases, they are your neighbors for years. You have to make choices about what your relationship with them will be—how will you interact with them, when will you help them, how will you respond to disputes? I've realized that the layout of your neighborhood plays a large role in how these relationships will be shaped.

On our particular dead-end street, the two-family homes did not have front yards. In fact, they barely had back yards. When I was a kid, the small back yards were places to run through, but not where anyone gathered or relaxed or even really stood still. Our houses were very close to each other, probably fifteen feet apart in many places. One would think that without yards and with close proximity, the neighborhood could easily become a

2. The Cambridge Historical Commissions' book on West Cambridge architecture describes houses along Brattle, Brewster, Highland, and Appleton Streets, seemingly from a "Brattle St. perspective." They talk about "...the avalanche of dense and rather monotone two-family dwellings" on the Appleton Road side of the hill. "The marked change of architectural quality on the North Slope is screened from view by that crest and by a slight deflection in the street's axis so that the pedestrian character of the buildings doesn't impinge on their more aristocratic neighbors."

tight-knit community where neighbors regularly chat and get to know each other well and maybe even begin to share responsibility for property and family. Then again, just around the corner on Appleton Street, there very were similar homes with similar traits—wouldn't you expect the same sense of community there?

Not necessarily. Because we lived on a dead end street, throughout my whole childhood, there was never any traffic to contend with, and this obviously gave us a lot of freedom of movement. Our particular neighborhood felt "contained" and so we could set it up any way we wanted. We could play in the street all day long, we could rake leaves and jump in the huge piles in the middle of the street, we could build massive snow forts in the winter—all while oblivious to cars traveling up and down Appleton Street or Huron Ave. Residents on those streets would be much less likely to call out to their neighbors across the street. Adults and kids certainly weren't able to gather in the middle of those streets, with the traffic a constant presence. But on a dead end, with no yards, with houses spaced so closely and with two families to a house, and with no traffic, all the ingredients were there for families to get to know each other and for kids to congregate and find things to do together. Anyone who grew up on a dead-end street probably had a similar experience. But we also had one unique feature on our short street that helped bring people together even more.

"Community, not privacy"

AROUND 1970, my parents and the Barton family next door agreed in writing that they would share the space between their houses (which at the time was just a dirt lot), using it as an outdoor gathering space rather than a driveway. The small terrace area—we always called it a "patio"—was half on the Barton property and half on the Beckwith property. It remained a shared space despite a landscaper telling the Bartons that they should plant trees or build a fence along the property line. The Bartons declined, explaining to the landscaper that what they wanted was "community, not privacy."

I didn't realize until decades later that this decision resulted in a somewhat unusual arrangement: a public street in the City of Cambridge that had a common open space for people from the neighborhood to gather, but which was not city property.[3] The idea worked. Kids from the neighborhood and kids who lived elsewhere would hang out with us in that spot, especially in the summer. Adults met there to barbecue or to just sit and talk or get respite from the summer heat under the crabapple tree. Every Memorial Day and Independence Day, a potluck is still held in that spot where as many as thirty people bring food and relax and catch up with each other. These gatherings have been annual events for at least forty years.

* * * * *

KIDS ALWAYS have friends "from the neighborhood"—as opposed to friends you know only from school—and so each neighborhood creates its own little ecosystem, a thriving, growing, ever-changing habitat made of people, places, pets, parents, and play.

Matthew and Patrick were brothers who lived right next door, so we saw them almost every day. Their basement ping-pong table and their magnetic football game were particular attractions, but they were involved in pretty much everything we did. Andrew (and sometimes siblings Jimmy and Amy or friend Craig) came by daily to visit with his grandmother and great aunt, who rented the downstairs apartment at our house, and together we played every outdoor and indoor game imaginable. Sarah, with

---

3. I told this story to an old friend from Cambridge and he said that he had lived in one of four row-house style homes that shared a common backyard, making for a huge recreational area for kids and adults. They agreed to maintain that shared yard for 30 years. When the 30 years were up and houses were sold, fences started going up. It is no more a shared backyard.

her mother and brother, lived in three different apartments on our little dead-end street over the years and was always part of all the activities. A whole set of siblings lived around the corner: Jackie, Betty, Patty, and Mary. Patty and Mary, being the youngest, always joined in our neighborhood games. I had a crush on both of them at different points, but especially on Mary. Megan[4], who had returned to the neighborhood from New Hampshire around sixth grade with her father Jeff, became my close friend up through all of high school and to this day. We spent time together listening to music, playing games, staying up all night talking, hanging out with our other friends, and chatting with her father, who wrote about music and the arts for the Boston Globe and related to (and tolerated) kids better than most parents.

Most of the neighborhood kids went to the public schools, but some attended Catholic or private schools. We didn't think about those differences—when you got home from school, you just knew who would be around to join in the latest adventure with. But something underlying my visits to different friends' houses stood out to me: when I'd go to a family's home that was different in some way from my own (heavily religious, poorer or richer, from a different cultural or ethnic or political background) I sensed that the "rules of the game" in that home would be different. I also knew that often I didn't yet know what those rules were.

Do you take your shoes off when you enter? Should I call your dad "Mr. Harney," or by his first name? Are kids allowed to grab a snack from the kitchen without asking permission? I'd try to observe as much as possible to see how each family behaved: what subjects they talked about and those they avoided, how the adults were addressed by the kids, and whether kids were allowed in adult areas. In many of the homes I visited, it became obvious that they weren't part of the bohemian/non-conformist world that I was used to in my home—there certainly wasn't a fist painted on the

4. Pronounced "MEE-gun," not "MEH-gun." Now you try it...

wall (there was, and still is, a 10-foot-tall blue raised fist painted on the wall of the stairway that takes you up to my parent's apartment—an abstract but direct statement by my parents about their values and belief system).

In noticing these differences, I also had a lingering question. Most of the kids I knew had families with some strong identity—they were Irish or African-American or Italian or Catholic—but what was I? I didn't define myself based on any ethnic or religious background. I didn't even really know that background when I was a kid. Instead, my family's identity was based more on the rejection of those labels and on beliefs about society, politics, and culture, which was not easy for a kid to process.

* * * * *

BEFORE THERE WERE "PLAYDATES," kids spilled out their front doors and onto the street—only then did we figure out what to do next. In the summer, we'd often be out on the street all day in bare feet. When it was hot, we'd run to the outside garden hose to get refreshed, slurping cold metallic-tasting water from the hose, and running right back to whatever game we were playing. If we had a quarter, we could take the bus into Harvard Square. If we had a bike, we could go anywhere we wanted with friends who also had bikes. It wasn't just that our parents didn't know what we were doing—often they didn't even know where we were. But there was usually one important rule that we needed to follow: "Be home for dinner!"

Andrew, Craig, Patrick, and I would spend time after school playing and trading with baseball cards. We had one game where we'd lean a bunch of cards against the bottom of a wall and then, from the other end of the room, fire cards at them almost like a frisbee until you knocked down all the leaning cards. We also played board games, read comic books, set up imaginary skirmishes with toy soldiers, drew pictures on construction paper, rode bikes (sometimes with a Radio Shack radio attached to my bike that could get the Red Sox games broadcasts), and played wiffle ball and football on the dead-end street for as long as we could get away with it. There was no internet, there were no computers to play games on, and watching TV wasn't even on the agenda—there were just too many other options!

The best and most complex outdoor game we played was *Relievio*. Two teams ran in and out of everyone's backyards and porches and down the street and around the corner, with the goal of capturing someone from the other team, holding them, and yelling "One two three, caught by me, no more Relievio powers!" If you did catch them, they'd go to the jail (the "patio"). To be "relieved," someone from the prisoner's team had to sneak past the jailer and tap them out, which was always pretty tricky to do.[5]

We also played classic kid games like hide and seek, sardines (the opposite of hide and seek, where one person hides and as each person finds them, they squeeze into the space with them—the last person to find them is the loser), four square, basketball (after getting a ladder and doing a very bad job of mounting a hoop on a leaning tree), football, street hockey, and wiffleball. We also did random things like leaving tiny secret folded-up messages in fence posts or under rocks for some sort of spy game or building a clubhouse in our dark, dusty, scary-looking basement and another inside an old refrigerator box in the alley behind the Zenith store around the corner.

Often, we'd just hang out on the small brick patio between the houses and talk about nothing and everything for hours. In a way, it was all random—there wasn't anything that was "scheduled." But in looking back, it seems like each activity was its own little opportunity to learn how different people behaved and

---

5. A quick web search finds an article on "*Relievio—A New England Street Game*" but deeper digging unearths a New York City-based game called Ringlevio, which is the same game, this one dating back to the late 19th century! How it got passed down from generation to generation is anyone's guess.

spoke and moved, to see how social contracts could be made and broken, to build community, and to test limits.

* * * * *

SOME MEMORIES STAY WITH YOU because you feel bad about something you did and you sense you should have known better at the time. One winter, when I was eleven or twelve, some friends and I thought it would be fun (or "funny"?) to stand on Appleton Street with our backs turned to the street and, as cars came down the hill towards Huron Ave, throw a snowball up in the air behind us to see if it would hit the car. It didn't take long for one of our snowballs to land—splat!—right on the windshield of one of those classic 1970s wood-paneled station wagons driving down the hill, with a large man behind the wheel. The car came screeching to a halt and started to back up, with the driver yelling something at us. We ran for our lives! I don't know where the other kids ended up, but I ran to the end of the dead end street, up a little alley on the side of the last house, and tucked myself behind a chimney as I listened in fear to the angry driver opening the car door, getting out, and looking for us.

Because we knew the neighborhood so well from all our games, it was pretty easy to find a hiding place where a stranger wouldn't find us, but I thought years later about what that incident shows about how undeveloped the adolescent (especially male) brain can be. To not realize how dangerous it would be to throw a snowball right at a driver's front windshield while the car is in motion—it's as if there's not yet room in the brain for thinking ahead, for calculating cause and effect, for taking into account the safety and security of others (and often yourself).

In fact, being just a few years older wasn't necessarily enough: when I was a freshman in high school, a friend and I were walking home after midnight along a deserted and quiet Concord Ave. We saw ahead of us one of those large blue U.S. mail collection boxes on the sidewalk and somehow we came to realize that it wasn't bolted down. Something put the idea into our head to lift the whole thing, carry it across the street, and place it down on the sidewalk directly opposite where it was supposed to be. We weren't thinking "...could this be a federal offense?," but instead "...boy, what I would give to see the look on the mailman's face the next day."

Getting to Work

BEING A KID, going to school and doing homework, finding things to do with friends—that's all fine, but at some point, a kid's gotta have some income. My parents would give me a weekly allowance of twenty-five cents for doing a few chores, like hauling out the trash or taking my weekly turn at making dinner for the family. Making a meal was a great idea, but I wasn't exactly a "top chef." I think I cooked boiled hot dogs and beef tacos for the family, but I know for sure that I made "English muffin pizzas," which are as bad as they sound. They were just English muffins with tomato sauce and melted cheese on them. I don't know how my parents put up with eating such a monstrosity. But that twenty-five cents didn't go far: I felt I needed money "of my own."

At around age twelve, I got my first job delivering the *Boston Herald American* newspaper to houses in my neighborhood, a job I kept for two or three years. I started with one small paper route and later added two or three other routes in other neighborhoods, eventually delivering up to 120 papers each morning. I'd first have to fold all the newspapers and then I'd put rubber bands around them, fill the employer-issued newspaper bag with the folded papers, and then—with the bag slung over my shoulder—hop on my bike and ride the streets, throwing the papers onto front stoops as I went.

It was hard getting up early each morning—my parents often had to drag me out of bed, even though that should have been my problem to solve. On Sundays, I would have to push a shopping cart with the much heavier newspapers in it. In the winter, with snow on the ground, delivering those Sunday papers with the shopping cart took forever.

Paper routes came in two flavors: a "collecting route" and a "non-collecting route." Mine was a collecting route, so every weekend I would have to walk around to all the houses with a little leather-bound booklet that held information on each home, what their weekly charge was, and a record of their past payments. I'd ring the bell of each home that I'd visited earlier that morning to collect their money, hopefully along with a nice tip. I learned from this process that the people at the top of the hill with the largest houses often gave the lowest tips (rounding a $1.90 bill to $2.00), and the ones at the bottom of the hill in two-family homes gave the best tips (rounding the $1.90 bill up to $2.50). I wondered, "*Is that why the people at the top of the hill are so rich? Because they aren't generous with their money?*" I can also still remember the smell of the home cooking of some of the houses I went to—I often had to go inside while they went to fetch the money. Some were elderly and wanted to make small talk with me, but I don't think I was receptive and was probably a bit afraid of them.

After collecting all the money, I'd go home, lay it out on the floor, add it all up, and figure out how much I had to give to the newspaper supplier and how much I would get for tips. When I first started, the guy I worked for ran his business out of the back of a van. He would set up shop on the weekend in a dirt parking lot on Sherman Street to collect the money from the paperboys (although girls did this job, too)—it was the same van they had used to deliver the batch of newspapers to all the kids early in the morning. Each weekend, I'd pull up on my bike at the back of the van, climb in, and go through the collections with the guy and his helper, all of us hunched down to avoid hitting the low ceiling of the van.

Eventually, the van guy moved his operation around the

corner into a downstairs apartment next to Masse's Hardware Store on Walden Street. One weekend, I pulled up as usual on my bike to the Walden Street location. I had to go inside the apartment and I wouldn't be able to see my bike from there. For some reason, on that day, I decided not to lock my bike. Maybe I forgot my lock and didn't feel like going back home. I leaned my bike up against the building and went inside. I remember thinking that I needed to get back outside quickly to make sure nothing happened to the bike, but other kids ahead of me were counting their money out and I had to wait.

By the time I was done and went back outside—you guessed it—my bike was gone. I looked down Walden Street and then ran to Sherman Street, trying to see the thief, but my bike was nowhere to be seen. I pictured the guy pedaling calmly down the street, laughing to himself at his luck in running into an unlocked, unattended bike right there on the sidewalk, leaning up against the apartment. That bike was gone forever and it made me very cautious for the rest of my life about locking my bicycle and being aware of my surroundings—although there was another close call with a bicycle theft during high school.

ONCE I STARTED working regularly, I had much more spending money: what should I do with it all? Beyond buying candy and saving some of the money, that extra cash helped me with some hobbies I had.

I have long been a "collector"—not a hoarder, but a careful collector of select items. I had a stamp collection at one point. I had a coin collection with special binders and little coin holders with circular windows. When I was twelve or thirteen, I would take the subway from Harvard Square into Boston, sometimes with friends, to buy coins or stamps or to sell some from our collections. In the 1970s, on old Bromfield Street near the MBTA Park Street station in Boston, there was an array of little shops that were geared towards collectors—all of them seemed to be run by hunched-over old men chomping on cigars like they were chewing on bitter memories of the "old country." There were stamp shops, coin shops, pen shops, watch repair shops, cigar shops, bookstores, antique shops, and several camera shops—it felt like an old European city scene.

When I was in fifth grade, I took a kid who I knew, but who wasn't a close friend, on one of these subway trips. His mother, who later became the principal of the Tobin School, told me after our trip that she was thankful that I gave her son an orientation on how to get around the city and use the public transportation system. Little did she know of what went on in "kid world" at the time.

I can't remember whether it was as we entered the subway at Harvard Square or when we exited at Park Street in Boston, but at some point, a group of kids started following us. I noticed them, but kept going about my business until the biggest one came up to me and said: "You wanna jam?" It took him repeating it a couple of times for me to figure out that he and his crew wanted to fight me and my friend. We turned down their generous offer, but they kept following and taunting us until we were able to duck into a shop and the tentative protection of an adult. We weren't sure how badly they wanted to get into it with us though, so we lingered extra long in the shop. Before leaving, we looked up and down the street several times to be sure they had given up and moved on with their lives.

I guess my collecting could also get a little weird at times. Around age ten, I was collecting discarded *bottle caps*—the ones that were once the crown on the top of soda and beer bottles. One of the best places to find these bottle caps was the old MBTA bus yards just outside of Harvard Square. At that point, the yards (where Harvard built the Kennedy School of Government several years later) had become a huge dirt parking lot. I'd wander around the lot, filling my pockets with any bottle caps I could find, probably not being all that careful to not pick up broken glass along the way. When I got home and emptied my pockets, about half of what came out was dirt from the lot, but that was the price I had to pay for a nice collection of caps. In our dark and musty basement, I kept two large boxes: one had a mix of caps from a variety of different brands of beer and soda, and the other was all *Schlitz* bottle caps, the lowest quality beer out there and the most common cap I would find. There was something about sorting through and categorizing them that drew me in—even though there was really no point to any of it. When I found a bottle cap with a brand that I'd never seen before, I thought of it as "rare," which made it more exciting.

With inspiration from Andrew and Patrick, I also started a baseball card collection (along with football, hockey and basketball cards). Each card had all the statistics for the player on the back, and we'd spend hours comparing stats and trading cards with friends. It didn't hurt that each pack of cards came with that long, flat, pink stick of gum with white powdered sugar and cornstarch on it.

But the most important collection to me—which is also the one that I held on to for the longest—was my comic book collection. I made regular trips to the Harvard Square shop *Million Year Picnic*[6], which had opened in 1974 as one of the country's first comic book specialty stores (before that, you'd have to go to a newsstand or drugstore magazine rack to buy the latest issues of your favorite comic). I collected mostly Marvel comics (*X-Men, Conan the Barbarian, Iron Fist*), but also some DC Comics (*Swamp Thing, Doctor Strange*) and others (*The Spirit*, published by Kitchen Sink Press at the time). After reading through my latest purchases, including reading the "letters pages" and checking out some of the strange advertising pages, I'd hand them over to my father. After he was done with them I'd put them in vinyl sleeves and store them in a comic book box until I wanted to read them again.

---

6. *Million Year Picnic* was named after a short story in Ray Bradbury's *The Martian Chronicles*.

Reading comic books for me was certainly escapism. While run-of-the-mill superheroes were cheap entertainment and some of the artwork and writing were not up to very high standards, many titles had deeper themes, beautiful artwork, and even complex dialogue—and I enjoyed it all. Since I wasn't much of a reader of books, I used comics to explore fantastical places, adventures in space, and real-world urban stories. But immersing myself in imaginary worlds didn't always prepare me for the real one.

After a few years of collecting comics, a friend from high school and I rented a table to sell part of our collections at the *ComicCon*—the comic book convention—at the Park Plaza Hotel in Boston. But before the doors opened to the public, while we were still getting our table set up, I noticed what appeared to be a veteran dealer slowly moving from table to table, surveying each person's offerings. When he got to our table, he paused to calmly look over our display. At first, he seemed uninterested and unimpressed. But after lingering for a moment, he offered me $30 for about twenty-five of my comic books (*X-Men* numbers 94 through 120). Wow—what good fortune! It made me feel like a big deal, for some adult dealer to be so interested in what I was selling. That is, until a few months later, when I saw that the value of those comics had started to shoot way up.

That dealer had known something that I hadn't: #94 was the start of the "New X-Men," where they were no longer in matching blue outfits and now had a wide diversity of heroes. This revolutionary new idea for an old comic was rapidly becoming extremely popular. Today, that single issue is worth $2,000-$5,000 in very good condition. What I learned from this experience was the power of "knowing what's going on" and how having inside information can be used by some people in vulturous ways against those who were, like me, clueless. Perhaps I got what I deserved.

I had another hobby when I was young that had nothing to do with collecting: "taking things apart." Dismantling a stereo to see the vacuum tubes and wires and resistors and capacitors, laid out like a chaotic small city. Taking a cassette player apart to see how those little wheels made the tape move smoothly past the playhead. Taking a transistor radio apart to try to fix a broken antenna. At some point, I got a Radio Shack electronics kit with components that could be connected in seemingly endless ways (a "100-in-1 Kit"). All I had to do was follow the instructions to get...*Flashing Lights! A Tone Generator! A Transistor Radio! An Electronic Bird! A Ticking Clock Sound! A Light Sensor! A Motion Sensor!* Working out the details of these circuits felt both scientific and magical; simultaneously logical and mystical. This habit of taking things apart, building things, and trying to understand how things work was an embrace of, and a fascination with, complexity, which would become a thread throughout my later life.

*****

I SOMETIMES WONDERED if the role of music in my home was out of the ordinary. Did the parents of other kids make listening to music a focus of their living room? Did other parents regularly play records on a turntable? Or cassettes on a tape deck? Did they tune into their favorite radio stations? What *kind* of music did they listen to?

In my case, both of my parents loved to listen to music and to dance to it and to collect it. Their collection ended up having a major influence on me later in life when I did some DJing in college and later hosted dancing parties and played music in bands.

They had a huge record collection, most of which is still intact. There was R&B (Stevie Wonder, Aretha Franklin, James Brown), rock (The Kinks, The Rolling Stones, The Talking Heads), folk (Dave Van Ronk, Bob Dylan, Woody Guthrie), reggae (Toots & the Maytals, Bob Marley and the Wailers, Jimmy Cliff), disco (The TRAMMPS, Donna Summer, Kool & the Gang), jazz (John Coltrane, Dave Brubeck, Thelonius Monk) classical (a genre I never really listened to or learned much about), and music from other genres or that crossed genres (Santana, Taj Mahal, Boy Ge Mendes, Cuban and French and Italian artists, an album of chain gang songs or protest songs).

Through their album collection, I picked up an appreciation of different cultures and came to understand the variety of ways people expressed themselves through music. I also learned how to take care of the vinyl albums and audio equipment: stripping the speaker wire ends and connecting them to the amplifier; operating the turntable, making sure it was level and keeping the needle clean; recording on the cassette deck and keeping the recording and playheads clean.

My parents also loved movies. Outings to a movie theater or to a drive-in were always a pleasure. Of course, at the time, there were no streaming services, no VHS or DVD movies to rent, and cable TV wasn't on our radar. Television stations didn't even show movies often, other than something like "The Movie of the Week." Fortunately for us, the Harvard Square Theater, within walking distance from our house, was innovative—they put out an oversized sheet every few months that listed all their "pairings" of movies. The films being shown changed daily and each day there was some connection between the films. You could pay one ticket price and stay to watch the two or three films on the marquee that day, back when most theaters had just one screen and hundreds of seats, including those in the balcony. One day they might have three Marx Brothers movies running, or two Humphrey Bogart movies or pairings like *M.A.S.H.* with *Airplane*, *The Shining* with *One Flew of the Cuckoo's Nest*, *Harold and Maude* with *King of Hearts*, or *North by Northwest* with *The Thin Man*.

The movie choices went beyond that, because Cambridge had several local venues for film: the Harvard Square Theater, the Brattle Theater, Fresh Pond Cinema, Orson Welles Cinema, the Central Square Theater, Off the Wall Cinema, and the Galleria Cinema. While I enjoy 2025's menu of streaming choices, there's no replacing the immersive experience of watching a film on a screen 65 feet wide and 30 feet tall. Most of the venues in the 1970s were also in old theaters that were built in a grand style, because "going to a show"—whether it was a play or musical or silent film in the early days—was the main and most important form of entertainment.

DESPITE my parents providing for me and raising me the way they did, I still did dumb things just like a lot of kids my age—things that were irresponsible and risky. But I suppose the riskiness was what made them attractive to young boys like me.

One such temptation was found in a small store up the street called Huron Drug—a locally-owned drugstore (as most were back then) that sold the usual band-aids and medicines but also had a candy counter up front, right by the register. I would walk home from school by heading up Standish Street, taking a left on Huron Ave and then passing by Huron Drug. I would often go in to buy candy, but something in me had a different idea. I would walk around for a bit and then hover around the candy counter, pretending to think carefully about whether to buy a chocolate bar or Pixy Stix or Fire Balls. What I was really doing was waiting for the owner to turn his back so I could slip a couple of candy bars into my pocket and walk out the door without paying for them.

Since I had an allowance when I was younger and a paper route when I was a little older, I don't think this was about an inability to pay for the candy.

I also recall buying firecrackers from some underground network of sellers. A lot of elementary school kids did this, despite the danger of the mini explosions that would occur whenever you lit them. My friends and I would ride around on our bikes at night and—with both hands off the handlebars to be able to hold the lighter and the firecracker—light firecrackers and throw them. While we never aimed them at people, but instead at the sidewalk or at a tree or into the street, I obviously wasn't carefully thinking through what I was doing and how it might affect people or property.

We simply experimented and learned what we could get away with and what we couldn't. I mean, what kind of a person would take a wiffleball bat to a log with a known bees nest in it, just to see what would happen? Yes, I did that. And I got stung several times as a reward. Lesson learned.

Inertia vs. Adventure

IN MY ADOLESCENT MIND, going to school and hanging with friends were the main events of life. On the other hand, when my *parents* wanted me to do something that *they* had planned, I often thought of it as getting in the way of whatever fun I imagined was happening with my friends. Somehow, the current activity I was engaged in was always better in my mind than the thing that would take me away from it. My father said I had "inertia."

Despite my resistance, my parents took my brother and me on several adventures. We went on camping and hiking and backpacking trips all across the country throughout the 1970s, including hiking into the Utah Canyonlands, camping in the White Mountains in New Hampshire, and backpacking in the San Juan Mountains in Colorado on a Sierra Club trip. We carried backpacks with sleeping bags and tents and water and clothes and food. I learned the "ways of the woods"—we followed trail blazes, melted snow in a cup for water, trudged up steep switchbacks, scrambled over boulders, survived unbearable heat, and learned to love gorp—even when it didn't have M&M's in it.

One trip we took when I was about eleven years old stood out so much that the family gave it a name: "*The Day We'll Never Forget.*" On that day, we planned to hike the Keet Seel trail—me, my brother Ben, my parents, and some friends of my parents. The Keet Seel trail leads to the Navajo Nations historic Keet Seel cliff dwellings in the Arizona desert. The seventeen-mile round-trip backcountry hike, with switchbacks, sand dunes, and river crossings is well-known as a strenuous and challenging one. The goal was to reach the historic site and camp out there for the night.

We were well-prepared with backpacks and tents and food, but we got started late (my parents' friends weren't as reliable as my parents had thought), we didn't have enough water for the trip, and it was blazing hot. We hiked for hours in long pants and long-sleeved shirts, carrying heavy backpacks—we were losing energy quickly. At one point, I was afraid we might not live to see the end of the day (looking back, we were certainly in danger of becoming badly dehydrated). After many stops to rest in the shade and to preserve our energy, we finally made it to the campsite, but found only a trickle of spring water. We eventually did get more water, we did set up camp, and we did make it out alive.

When I look back now at these adventures that I was always trying to get out of, they did give me a physical challenge that I probably needed. They got me to take in the beauty of nature in a way that was important for a kid growing up in a city. They also opened my eyes to what other parts of the country looked, felt, smelled, and sounded like. And they likely laid the groundwork for my own crazy outdoor excursions as an adult.

Me, Barbara, and Ben at Keet Seel

"I made it to the top!" c.1977

5

HI, SCHOOL

ON SEPTEMBER 8, 1978, kids from all around the city converged at what is pretty close to the geographical center of Cambridge to attend the first day of school at *Cambridge Rindge and Latin School* (CRLS), the city's only public high school[1]. The 1977 merger of two schools—*Rindge Technical School* and *Cambridge High and Latin School*—into CRLS meant that 2,900 teenagers from every conceivable background and every location in the city would be together in one building[2]—White, Black, Hispanic, Asian, working class, wealthy, academically-oriented, and those going into the trades. The merger was still happening, so most of us still had classes in the deteriorating red brick Latin building while we waited for the completed CRLS building to open.

I met Carol in a study hall in the Latin building. She was talkative and easy to get to know. Every Monday during third period, we would go to a large room for our study hall—which in this

1. The lower grades in Cambridge at the time were a K-8 system, unlike many school systems that have middle schools or junior high schools, so kids went straight from their elementary schools to high school.
2. The population of Cambridge at the time was about 95,000.

case actually was in a "hall." To me, it was mysterious—a cavernous room, seemingly neglected for years, with tall ceilings and white fluted columns at the front that had carved busts (ones that seemed way too formal for the space) atop each of the columns. The hall had a wide open floor and two sets of rows of student desks, all facing a small teacher desk at the front, which felt out of place in what seemed more like a venue for a theatrical event.

On those Mondays, I would notice Carol a few desks in front of me, looking through the *Boston Globe* newspaper. Eventually, we got to know each other and I learned she was looking at the newspaper for the horse racing results from the night before, which kind of added to her mystique. By the second half of our freshman year, Carol and I had become friends.

That spring of 1979, Carol and I, and a friend named Mario, were eating lunch outside near the under-construction part of the new building when Carol blurted out, "Let's go check out the new building!" There were a couple of problems with this plan. The first was that the new building wasn't open yet and we weren't allowed in a building still under construction. The second and third problems were that we all had a class to go to and none of us had ever cut a class in high school–yet. For whatever reason, we decided it would be worth it (Carol could be very persuasive), and so we found our way around to the side entry door and cautiously tried the handle. To our surprise...it opened!

We peered inside to see plastic covering on parts of the stairs that were finished and needed protection, areas of unfinished floor tiles, and loose wiring coming out of the ceiling. The three of us crept in through the door, but then saw that there were construction workers in the area. At that point, we probably should have turned around, left the building, and gone to class. But instead, we decided to act like we belonged there, and just walked right in. Hearing no objections from the workers, we turned and climbed the new stairs, with their dark purple rubber treads, to the second floor and emerged through the double doors to discover what the new building had to offer us. It was worth it.

The walls were pure white and contrasted with the long rows of lockers that had alternating rainbow colors and which lined a slowly curving hallway. We walked down the empty halls in silence, running our hands along the lockers. We had never seen anything like it. It was clean, fresh, and modern, compared to the dirty and dingy feeling of the old building, with its heavy windows, beat-up lockers, and dark stairways. Even more than our amazement at the sight before us, the three of us felt an exhilaration for having pulled off an illegal entry into a massive unfinished building that it seemed like we had all to ourselves up on the second floor. We weren't competing with the upperclassmen or looking out for teachers or thinking about homework or wondering what was for lunch. We were wandering in the wilderness.

*****

THE EVENTUAL TRANSITION to the new combined high school building seemed to go smoothly for both students and teachers. The building was everything it promised to be: it had a new look, a new feel, and a new smell, even though it was contained within the old bones of the original 1932 structure. It still had the large classrooms, hallways, and stairwells of the original building, but with newly-installed lights, paint, floors, and ceilings. All of this, combined with a new and modernized cafeteria, gym, main office space, auditorium, and computer labs, made for a much better high school experience than the falling-apart and dangerous Latin building could provide.

*****

THERE WERE THREE WAYS FOR ME TO GET TO SCHOOL. I could walk there (about 1.5 miles), mostly a straight shot down

Concord Ave, followed by a diagonal cut through the Cambridge Common (a big hippie hangout in the 1960s and 1970s), and then a short stint on Broadway, taking me right to CRLS. Walking would take about half an hour, with plenty of sights and sounds to entertain me along the way (I would often walk to school with my neighbor Megan, making the trip even more entertaining—for both of us). Another approach would be to ride my bike along that same route, cutting the time down to about ten minutes, including a nice long downhill on Concord Ave (which would turn into a long uphill on the way home). Lastly, I could walk around the corner from my house and wait for the #72 Huron Ave bus to do most of the work for me. The 72 was a trackless trolley bus that dropped its passengers off in the tunnel at the Harvard Square MBTA station, so I would emerge from the tunnel into the morning sun, cut through Harvard Yard to Broadway and walk two more blocks to the high school. (I don't think in my four years of high school I was ever driven to school.)

I do recall that I chose the walking mode on my very first day of high school, because the walk home at the end of that day is still seared into my memory.

Back in those days, there was a "tradition" that some of the older kids would follow on that first day of school. Once the final bell rang to end the day and the kids spilled out of the various doors on their way to the different parts of the city, the older kids would begin chasing down any freshmen they could find and either giving them a beating or stealing their shoes or tearing off their shirt. This was called "freshman initiation"[3], but it was really just an opportunity to exact some cruelty on a vulnerable population (it was not sanctioned by the school, obviously). On that first day, after going to the first meeting of all my classes (Algebra, English, History, Spanish, Earth Science, and BASIC programming), I headed out through one of the doors on the

3. It seems like this hazing/harrassment practice ended by about 1990.

Broadway side of the building to avoid leaving through the main entrance, thinking I would be more inconspicuous that way.

I remember leaving the building, crossing the street, and walking down Broadway heading west, carrying my notebooks at my side. As I walked down the bumpy red brick sidewalk, I kept my eye out to see if anyone was coming for me. When I turned to glance behind me, I saw a kid I'd known from Tobin School race towards me at top speed. Once he reached me, he flew right past, followed by three or four older boys chasing after him. The kid was pretty fast and I wasn't sure they were going to catch him, but I realized that they had just passed by me, a perfectly good slow-walking freshman—why?

The kid they were chasing was probably 5'3," but luckily for me, I'd had my entire growth spurt before I entered high school and so I was already my full height of about 5' 10 ½". Walking home, I realized that they had probably assumed, because of my height, that I was an upperclassman and so they never thought of me as a target. I think it also helped that I tried not to show any fear—the only way to decide who is a ninth-grader is to know the kid personally or to assume that they are a freshman either because they are small or because they are feverishly running away from you after school. The student they chased by me that day joined the track team later that year and I never ended up being a target of the freshman initiation. I did, however, wind up in a couple of skirmishes at school during my freshman year.

Each incident was as brief as it was illogical and neither resulted in any bumps or bruises. The first happened as I was on my way to a class in the old Latin building. I remember approaching the old, large wooden classroom door with paned glass on the top half, trying to get to class on time. I had just come up the stairs and a row of lockers were on my right. As I approached the classroom door, Gregory—for reasons I cannot understand to this day—decided he would knock the books and notebooks I was carrying out of my hands with a swipe of his arm. As the books tumbled to the floor, my reflexes took over and

I watched as my right arm swung up from my side, right at him. It was fast enough that I didn't even have time to close my fingers into a fist, instead whacking him in the side of the head with an open palm, which resulted in knocking him to the tiled floor. As I recall it, there was no decision-making on my part; my mind just told my arm what to do without asking me. I picked up my books and continued on into class, wondering if this would end up escalating. But I don't recall any lingering feelings between Greg and myself—it was just a strange, aggressive moment that apparently faded as quickly as it occurred—but not from my memory.

The other incident occurred later that year, this time in what was the old part of the Rindge building, where I had one or two of my classes. For some reason, there was a kid in that class who wanted to get into a fight with me (I think he had been itching to do so for a while). We were sitting in the back of the classroom and I definitely didn't do anything to antagonize him—I didn't even know who he was. He got up, walked over to my desk, and tried to take a swing at me, which I ducked away from. Then I stood up and we both started flailing at each other, but before anything could connect, a teacher came in to break it up (the kid was big and looked pretty tough, so I'm fortunate none of his punches landed).

Why does a kid do something like that? As an adult, I would consider what inadequacy this kid might have felt that inspired him to find someone that he wanted to physically assault and assert his dominance over, but I really have no idea. The interesting footnote to this story is that the fight resulted in my being sent to the main office where Mr. George Greenidge (the football coach and some kind of informal assistant principal) was tasked with "setting me straight." I tried to tell him I hadn't started it and was not someone who gets into trouble, but he walked with me to the outside the building, where he took me for a drive in his little red sports car with the roof down, apparently to give me words of wisdom and convince me to "stay out of trouble" in the future. I didn't need it, but I wonder if he also took my attacker for a similar ride and if that approach would have gotten through to him.[4]

*****

BY 1978, I had outgrown delivering newspapers for a living and so at the age of fourteen, I got a job at the main branch of the Cambridge Public Library, about 100 feet from the front entrance of the high school (my "commute" after school was about a minute). The library was housed in a Romanesque building constructed in 1888.[5] At first, my work involved just maneuvering a cart of returned books through the aisles and putting them back on the shelf in the right spot according to either the author's name or the Dewey Decimal system. As with any job, there were parts I enjoyed and parts I didn't.

As I wheeled the cart around the library and through the aisles, I would often come upon homeless people in ragged clothes and smelling of urine who were sleeping on benches or between bookshelves. I felt bad for them, but also had no sense of how to deal with them, so I just did my job, knowing that it was "above my pay grade" to do anything more than that. Churches, train stations, and libraries tended to be places of refuge for people whose problems were big enough that they had nowhere else to go—and this is still true today.

Eventually, I was needed elsewhere in the library. I got put into a back room tucked away "in the stacks" to be the person in charge of the magazine archives. "The stacks" were a dark and cavernous three-story area in the back of the library, with huge

---

4. Greenidge was a Cambridge institution before that incident in 1978 and for many years after. In 2024, when Greenidge was 83 years old, football players, assistant coaches, and cheerleaders connected to his 38 years as football coach had a gathering in Central Square to recognize his influence on their lives.

5. Before that, the main branch of the CPL had shared a building with the old city hall for a few decades. The new Cambridge City Hall in Central Square was also built around 1888, and in the same style as the 1888 library.

sets of shelves for all the books that weren't in the main part of the library. The floors were open iron grids, so you could see through to the floors above and below. My job was to organize all the magazine archives and when someone submitted a written request for a specific back issue of some newspaper or journal or magazine, I would fetch it for them and bring it to the front, emerging from the darkness into the well-lit library.

There were times when I didn't really have much to do back there, so since I was out of sight (and hearing) of the rest of the library, I started to bring in my medium-sized boombox to play tapes of my favorite music (funk/R&B) or listen to WILD/1090AM while I worked. There was definitely something exciting about being in a library and playing music where no one could hear it—and it certainly made the job more bearable, although looking back, I think my bosses wouldn't have approved.

*****

I'VE BEEN TOLD by several people over the years that I'm a "good listener," which I think has translated into it being easier for me to make friends with girls (as a kid) and women (as an adult) than it sometimes is for other guys. But when you're a teenager, being able to easily make friends with girls is quite different from knowing how to take a relationship in a romantic direction. While I did go on some dates with girls in high school, I would remain clueless about the "rules of romance" for quite a while. But at least I had lots of great friends.

I had been close friends with my next-door neighbor, Megan, since the sixth grade. We shared music with each other, went to school together, hung out at each other's houses (mostly hers), went to the movies, and talked about anything and everything. Her father was an arts writer for the *Boston Globe* and as a result of his position, their house was filled with thousands of records of every imaginable genre that he was given to review. Megan was a music connoisseur and through her I got exposed to so much good new music that never would have otherwise been on my radar. Her house was also the "cool place to hang out" for several of our high school friends.

In high school, Megan had made friends from other parts of the city, some of whom became my good friends. There were also kids that I met in classes or at lunch or through other friends who were from other parts of the city—especially kids from Cambridgeport or East Cambridge, places that were geographically still kind of mysterious to me and had significant Portuguese, Cape Verdean, Italian, and Haitian populations.

*****

THE CLASSES I HAD AT CRLS varied in how engaging they felt for me. I felt like some of the English and Social Studies classes were taught by teachers who didn't really have a passion for their subject, and so, probably as a result, I ended up with none. I will admit, however, that since I was a tinkerer—more of a math and computer science kid than a humanities kid—it might have been a bit tougher to get me inspired by humanities courses. I definitely had one great English teacher (Ms. Kervick, who ended up teaching at CRLS for more than three decades) who was friendly yet serious and was engaging, knowledgeable, and inspiring. I took difficult science classes, but they did not come easily to me, despite my father being a passionate microbiologist. It was in my math and computer programming classes that I found my sweet spot. I loved the problem-solving and complexity they required and I thrived on the process of writing and refining code to accomplish some real-world task.

When I was in high school, the term "PC" to refer to the idea of a "personal computer" barely existed. This is because computers at the time were generally large machines that existed in businesses, government institutions, and schools. The idea of a computer that a regular person could own at home and use by themselves (without having to build it themselves) didn't fully catch on until the early 1980s, with the advent of the *Commodore 64*, *AppleII*, and Radio Shack's *TRS-80*. However, one of the advantages of going to school in Cambridge was the proximity to, and relationship with, local colleges and universities.

In the case of CRLS, the high school was able to offer computer programming courses starting in the mid- to late-1970s (earlier than many schools across the country) by connecting to a "mainframe" computer, housed at the Massachusetts Institute of Technology.[6] There were no actual computers in the computer lab at the high school—instead, there were rows of VT100 monitors with keyboards attached. The monitors were just black screens with white or green text staring out at you, and since the computer mouse would not become popular for a few more years, everything was controlled through typing on the keyboard. Whatever you typed was sent as data to the mainframe computer at MIT, which would do all the work and then send data back to appear on our screens—that's how we wrote our programs.

The programming courses I took were taught by two new young teachers—Ms. Rehfield and Mr. McGlathery—and I signed up for all the courses I could, taking four courses over four years (BASIC, COBOL, Fortran, and Assembly Language Programming). I would often spend time after school with friends, working on fun programs like creating a phone book or making a text adventure game. The complexity of writing the code, debugging to find the mistakes, and then getting feedback from seeing everything appear on the screen was part of the magic for me. This was not memorizing dates and names or even mathematical formulas or biology terms—it was *taking action* and doing something logical and complicated that resulted in a clear reward when I got the thing to work.

I soon joined the Computer Science team and Math team at CRLS—both coached by Ms. Rehfield (although I believe the

---

6. The connection was made by coaxial cables going the mile or so down the road to the university.

aptly-named Mr. Wisdom was in charge at some point). Our team competed in the *New England Computer Science League*[7] finals in 1981 in Rhode Island, where we had to answer intricate contest questions about computer science concepts and then write large and complex programs as a team to achieve some specified result. The team came in second overall in the finals and we all got trophies. But honestly, I was not the top tier of this coding team—my teammates were brilliant. Their coding was elegant and their ability to quickly grasp the essence of a problem and solve it was impressive. One of them later went on to a job at Microsoft and another became a professor at MIT.[8]

But for me, all this "computer science stuff" wasn't really work: it was fun. Just like someone who is passionate about a sport might look forward to going to practice instead of dreading it, I always looked forward to the after-school work I did, which involved collaboration, laughter, and excitement.

* * * * *

FOR MOST OF MY LIFE, I had not been a reader of books. I did read a lot of *comic* books, but until 1980 (when I was 16), I had never read a book that helped me understand the power of reading; that showed me how a carefully-crafted piece of literature could give the reader a depth of understanding that short-form writing would always lack. The first book I ever read that opened my eyes to this reality was the actor Sidney Poitier's autobiography *This Life*, which had just come out. The book told of Poitier's young life on Cat Island in the Bahamas, living with no plumbing or electricity. It continued through to his arrival in New

7. The league was formed just 3 years earlier, in 1978, and is still going strong as of 2025, but has long since become the American Computer Science League.

8. I still get together with some of these (now) men and women, for a poker game in Cambridge every few months, including my old friends Paul, Patrick and Wati, along with friends I met in high school: Ned, James, Sarah, Jason, Philecia, and Andrew

York City, his discovery of acting, and his rise to becoming one of the great American actors of his time and one of the most important African-American actors in history (in the book, he also reflected on his personal life, marriages, and children). I had already been enamored of his films at that point, so reading the details of how he came to be that man and what life was like growing up in the Caribbean—*this* was what I wanted in a book. It didn't feel like some kind of an assignment: the fine details of his life felt more real than any of what I got from the history books I had been assigned to read.

In fact, Sidney Poitier felt like a bit of a hero to me. There was a set of public figures at the time that I was finding myself drawn to, which included Poitier along with the Afro-Panamanian Minnesota Twins baseball player Rod Carew, who flirted with batting .400 in more than one season; Chaka Khan, the powerful Chicago-born singer and musician; the singer Stevie Wonder, whose powerful lyricism and songwriting were beyond compare; and Thurgood Marshall, who sat on the Supreme Court at the time. For some reason, I generally felt a pull from African-American public figures. I was impressed by them and looked up to them and felt like I had something to learn from them—something that the "White world" often could not teach me. I felt a similar connection with the kids I went to school with, and it was likely this feeling that manifested itself later in life when I became heavily involved in the Boston and Cambridge reggae music scene.

*****

THE MAIN ACTIVITIES that consumed my free time in my early years of high school were doing school work, listening to music, hanging out with friends, riding bikes, and playing pinball.

I had met Bobby in my freshman year and we had quickly become friends. He was an athlete, he was smart, and he hard a biting sense of humor. One of the main things we did together after school was to go to local restaurants and cafés to play pinball. In the 1960s, the City of Cambridge had put severe restrictions on licensing pinball machines to restaurants and had completely blocked allowing any "amusement arcades" from coming into Cambridge. At the time, pinball machines and other coin-operated amusements were seen as connected to organized crime (the Route 2 Bowladrome had even taken the city to court over the licensing issue).

I became quite good at pinball and Bobby and I had a nice rivalry going, although his skills were always a notch above mine. Each place we went to play pinball, in and around Harvard Square, had different machines and a different vibe. *Elsie's Lunch* on Mt. Auburn Street was a very busy Jewish-style delicatessen with green-colored sawdust on the floor and there was always a huge lunch crowd, pushing up against the counter to get their orders in. *Rendezvous* on Holyoke Street was a Vietnamese restaurant and bar with two or three machines in the dark back room, some of them from the late 1960s. *Tommy's Lunch* on Mt. Auburn Street was an old-style sandwich joint with grumpy cooks. It had tall-backed booths that were usually populated by interesting characters. Tommy's had one pinball machine tucked away by the back door. *The Sandwich Shop* on Church Street had just one old pinball machine: *Flip-Flop*, made by Bally. Of all of those places, Tommy's was the only one that I and other friends of mine would order food and would just hang out for hours at a time. One of the cooks there was named Bob and I later worked with him at a deli a few blocks away.

But the best place of all for pinball, along with the new arcade games that were being developed, was *1001 Plays*[9], which had opened on Mass. Ave. between Harvard Square and Central Square in the fall of 1977. It was a huge space right in the middle of the city and was filled with all kinds of machines. Bobby and I

9. *1001 Plays* was later renamed/rebranded "*America's Game*," taking all the fun right out of the title.

(as well as many other friends) spent hours and hours there, honing our skills not just on the pinball machines, but on the new arcade games like *Asteroids*, *Space Invaders*, *Joust*, and *Defender*. Bobby and I both got good enough at pinball and arcade games that we could put one quarter in and end up making it stretch for hours, often walking away and gifting whatever credits we had racked up to the next person in line. We both competed in the 1981 Cambridge Pinball Championship. Bobby got further than I did, but it was hard to compete against the adults.

Compared to today's online or phone-based games, playing pinball and arcade games back then was a completely different experience. First of all, you had to have a job to earn the money to have the quarters to play the games. Secondly, you had to leave your house and travel somewhere (usually by bike, sometimes by bus) to play the games, getting some exercise and some sun along the way. Lastly, you had to interact *in person* with all kinds of other people, because you were either waiting to play a machine, or someone was waiting for you to finish.

There was a system: if you wanted to play a game that someone else was already playing, you would wait until just the right time when it wouldn't distract the current player and then carefully place one quarter on the lower part of the glass of the pinball machine or the lower part of the plexiglass of the video game display. This didn't mean that when the person finished their current game, you could take over, though. If they'd won several extra games, you might have to wait until they used up all of those games—but the unwritten rule was that if they lost, they wouldn't put a new quarter in, and it was your turn—although the two of you might agree to a two-player game. The people you had this (usually silent) negotiation with were sometimes kids and sometimes adults. Some were city kids and others were college students. There were graduate students and bus drivers and everything in between. They were from different parts of Cambridge or from out of town. That process of negotiating with these strangers probably helped kids like me become more comfortable with different types of people later in life.

On one of my visits to "1001" (as we all called it), I was very glad to have had one of my old friends from Tobin School with me. Paul and I had biked there after school and, after playing a few games, went across the street to get a snack (for me it was always a cookie, with my lifelong sweet tooth taking over the decision-making process). I was sitting at a table, facing the inside of the store. Paul was on the other side, facing out to the street. Just as I was taking a big bite out of the huge chocolate chip cookie, Paul, without saying a word, jumped up and ran out of the place. I sat there with the half-eaten cookie in my open mouth, wondering what was going on, but I wasn't sure what to do, so I took that bite and sat there, waiting for him to come back. When he didn't, I got up and went out onto the street.

I looked left down Massachusetts Ave in the direction of Harvard Square—no Paul. I looked right towards Central Square and there he was, about 50 yards down the street. But he was not alone. As I ran towards the two figures, I saw that they were both holding onto something...what was it?

Hey, that's my bike!

I had locked my beloved red Raleigh Record Ace to one of the bike racks in front of 1001 Plays. The problem was that I had locked only the front wheel, a rookie mistake.

A kid I only half knew from high school, Joey, must have taken an adjustable wrench and simply unscrewed the bolts on the locked front wheel (I didn't have quick-release on this bike—did anyone back then?) and lifted the rest of the bike from the rack. As he headed down Mass Ave with the stolen front-wheel-less bike, he had passed right in front of the shop where Paul and I were sitting. Paul had seen Joey with my bike and reacted by jumping up and running after him. When I ran up to them, they were both holding onto the bike and arguing. When Joey saw me, he calmly said, "Let me fight *him* for the bike."

Joey didn't want to fight Paul, who was an athlete and significantly more muscular than I, but Paul obviously wasn't going to go for the deal Joey was offering. Thanks to Paul, I got the bike back and that was the last time I locked only my front wheel. It was also the closest I ever got to losing that bike: I still have it (well, the frame) in my basement, forty-eight years after buying it and forty-five years after almost losing it that day.

Tensions Across Cambridge

AFTER WINTER VACATION in my sophomore year, CRLS had a short academic week, with students returning to classes after the break on Wednesday, January 2, 1980. We reconnected with friends and got back to work in our classes. The following weekend was uneventful—but on the following Monday, January 7, 1980, all hell broke loose.

Anthony Colosimo was a 17-year-old senior at CRLS from East Cambridge who played guitar and harmonica and who was becoming more interested in reading the Bible—but he also sometimes got into fights.[10] He had two older sisters and an older brother. Colosimo had apparently gotten into some kind of beef with another student the week before and whatever the issue was between them, it erupted into a fight on that Monday. The fight started in an area just outside the unfinished new Arts building and then it escalated. During the fight, 16-year-old William Tasco joined in—but he had a knife. Tasco ended up stabbing Colosimo as well as Colosimo's friend, 18-year-old William Graham. Colosimo died later that day as a result of his injuries. (There was a rumor going around the school at the time that Tasco was from Boston, but as I researched to write this story, I learned he was a CRLS student.)

People across Cambridge were horrified and saddened by the violence and the tragedy. Many in Cambridge were also

---

10. His mother described him this way in a Cambridge Chronicle article in January of 1980.

concerned that the incident might exacerbate racial tensions in the city, since the victims, Colosimo and Graham, were White and Tasco and his friends were Black. However, newspaper interviews from the time show that most thought that despite the racial makeup of those involved, the cause of the fight was not related to race. The major concern was that the incident would lead to more fights around the city, but in the two nights following the murder, police reported no increase in violence.

The killing did, however, start serious conversations across the city about existing racial tensions. It also led to the shutting down of the school, from Tuesday, January 8, until the following Monday, January 14. When we returned to school, the most obvious change was that, for the first time, the school had employed security guards, who were on the lookout for violence or trouble of any kind, and there were uniformed officers positioned outside of the school. The security guards would become a part of the school environment for years to come.

My memory of this time was that there was a lot of tension in the school because of what had happened, but also that kids still got along with each other and I don't recall any increase in fear of further violence. It might have been a different experience for me if I had personally known any of the five students involved, but I didn't. And like many traumatic events that occur in society, eventually things seemed to me to "get back to normal."

But the range of reactions to the incident was complex and mixed. Two days after Anthony Colosimo's death, his father, Edward, told the *Cambridge Chronicle* that he hoped his son's death would not lead to increased tensions at the high school. The *Chronicle* article reported Edward as saying: "It wasn't a racial thing. I don't know. It could be deep down, but more violence won't prove anything." Anthony's mother, Marie, said that Anthony had gotten involved in fights—"he was that type of kid"—but only fistfights and never with weapons.

By the next day, the family had already decided that they

wanted donations in Anthony's memory to go towards a college scholarship fund for CRLS students.

Tasco was eventually charged and convicted of manslaughter. But because he was a juvenile, he was released from detention just two years later when he turned 18. This, along with the fact that Tasco had escaped from the Chelmsford juvenile detention center in August of that year without any additional charges being filed, enraged Colosimo's parents, who wrote letters to the editor looking for justice. As far as I can tell, Tasco never faced further punishment for the murder of Colosimo beyond those two years served.[11]

Was there racial tension in Cambridge in those years? Why was it so easy for some to see this as a Black/White issue rather than just a stupid fight gone tragically wrong? In the weeks following the incident, some Black students in Cambridge and their parents were quoted in the newspaper as being concerned about the racism they'd experienced coming from some of their teachers and some of their White peers at the school. These concerns were legitimate, and yet I think the majority of teachers were aware of these issues and at least attempted to deal with their students in an unbiased way. Some White students and their parents were concerned about some Black kids harassing or beating up some White kids. These concerns were also legitimate, and yet I think the majority of White and Black kids got along well, even if there were some tensions.

---

11. I did some research and found a reference to Tasco as living in Alabama in 1982. I then found a 1990 article about a William N. Tasco graduating in 1987 from a N. Carolina college and then becoming a member of the National Guard (the graduation year fits with the age of the Cambridge William Tasco). It also listed this William Tasco's mother as Geraldine Tasco. I found a 1967 listing showing Geraldine Tasco filing for divorce from her husband William A. Tasco in Cambridge (presumably the younger William Tasco's father). The reason given for the divorce was that William was incarcerated and would continue to be for the next 5 years. So I am pretty confident that the 1990 article is the same William Tasco from CRLS and that he never returned to jail and in fact may have turned his life around by attending college and joining the National Guard.

I suspect that most White kids in Cambridge had good friends who were Black and vice versa, and that in many cases there was affection and mutual respect between them. This doesn't mean that everyone got along with everyone else—there were plenty of negative Black-White interactions where race was perceived as playing a major role in them. When I graduated two years later, it was with pride and with love for my school and the students in it. I had become friends with a wide variety of kids, but I knew from all my years in Cambridge that—just like anywhere in America—it is hard to escape issues of race, bias, conflict, justice and injustice. But for the most part, there is no way to judge individuals unless you get to know them personally and there were plenty of opportunities in Cambridge to do just that.

*****

YOU KNOW how people love to claim a famous person as "one of their own" just because that person lived in their town or went to their school—or they ran into them at a gas station one day? Well, I am not immune to this "claim to fame" urge. At times, I thought it made me special that I went to school with Patrick Ewing, the Cambridge kid who eventually became the center for the New York Knicks (and later a coach at Georgetown) and is considered one of the greatest centers in NBA history. But how does his greatness make *me* special? It doesn't. Even if I were friends with him, I'm not sure how that would make me a more interesting person. I did have an English class with him in my sophomore year and he sat behind me and tapped me on the shoulder a few times to ask me questions about the work we were doing. Friends of mine would sometimes see him near Central Square riding a moped with his lanky knees sticking way up in the air. But that was about the extent of my personal interaction with him.

Pat was born in Jamaica and came to Cambridge in his adolescence, having never touched a basketball. By the time he was in high school, he was already approaching 7 feet tall and his basketball skills were rapidly developing. He could be found at Hoyt Field or Corporal Burns Park shooting hoops whenever he found the time, but ultimately, it was expert coaching that helped him hone his skills. Here's how he brought greatness to Cambridge basketball: the team had 94 wins and 5 losses during his four years of playing center for CRLS, including going 77-1 in his last three years and winning three state titles in a row. These successes resulted in ranking CRLS the best basketball team in the country for a time.

I don't recall how many games I attended, but I do remember attending the last game with Patrick Ewing in 1981—the championship game, the epic game against Boston College High School, which took place on a Boston University basketball court. As was often unavoidable in Boston in those days, there was a racial element to that game. The BC High fans (not necessarily the players) behaved terribly.[12] To set the scene, on one side of the gym was what appeared to be a 100% White male crowd backing the BC High team. It was a boys' school and all of the BC High players were White. On the CRLS side, the crowd was a mix of Black, White, Hispanic and other cultures. The CRLS team was made up of all Black players. While there was nothing inherently wrong or controversial about the makeup of those teams, there were two things that stuck out to me that night.

The first thing was the style (or lack thereof) of the fans. On the BC High side, there was a monotone chant they did in support of the team, that went like this:

"B!"
"C!"
"High!"

---

12. A 2021 Facebook post by members of that BC High team 40 years later lamented the fact that their fans' behavior overtook the narrative, which should have been about one of the greatest basketball teams BC High ever put on the court.

Pause.
"B!"
"C!"
"High!"
Pause.
Repeat...

On the CRLS side, we had a melodious chant in support of the team that went like this:

"We!"
Claps.
"Are!"
Claps.
"The mighty, mighty, Warriors!"
Claps.
"And we!"
Claps.
"Don't give!"
Claps.
"A hoot about you!"
Two Claps.
Repeat...

Okay, so their fans weren't creative and ours were—not a big deal. But once the BC High team started losing the game, the fans started yelling insults at Pat Ewing, referencing his intelligence and comparing him to an ape. It was disgusting. The chant in particular that I remember was "You can't read! You can't read!" Not only was it a childish insult, but of course Pat went on to be a great basketball player and to coach at the college level for years. I suspect that Pat being from Jamaica and having a Jamaican accent was what spurred these rival fans to charge him with a lack of intelligence, instead exposing their own.

The revenge was sweet: CRLS beat BC High easily, winning 87-58 and walking away with the trophy. It was a small miracle that a huge brawl didn't break out that night, and that was a testament to the classiness of our fans and the greatness of our coach, Mike Jarvis.

So, no, I didn't contribute in any way to Pat's success and wasn't even a friend of his. But it was still a point of pride for me and my classmates to have been a part of a school with such a historic team and to have been around one of the NBA greats *before* he became famous.

A CRLS hallway after the building received a more recent renovation - the rainbow-colored lockers are no more

The 1981 CRLS boys basketball team from the yearbook.
Pat Ewing is in the back, center

6

NEW LESSONS FROM TAKING THINGS APART

One Scoop, or Two?

WITH EVERY NEW JOB came new challenges. In my junior year of high school, at the dawn of the 1980s, I got a job at *Bailey's Ice Cream* right in the middle of Harvard Square, at 21 Brattle Street (my friend Bobby already worked there and probably helped me get the job).

Bailey's ice cream parlor and sandwich shop had been a Boston-area institution since 1873. If you walked in the front door of the Harvard Square Bailey's in 1980, you would have seen a soda fountain behind a long old-fashioned wooden counter where sandwiches, ice cream, and milkshakes were served to hungry customers. On the left, you'd take in the enticing spectacle of a long, wood and curved-glass candy counter with a wide variety of candies and chocolates carefully arranged to be irresistible to any fellow sweet-toothers like me. Straight ahead past the counters, you'd see a scattering of small round marble-top tables, with classic "ice cream parlor chairs"—the ones with curly iron backs which somehow indicated that "sweet cold things are eaten here." I suspect the place looked much the same fifty years earlier.

If you came back a few times, you might eventually notice another antiquated aspect of Bailey's Ice Cream Shoppe, as I did after working there for a week or so: they hired exclusively female employees for that candy counter on the left and only male employees for the ice cream/sandwich counter on the right. I wondered at the time how they got away with that (the Civil Rights Act of 1964 should have prevented it). Hopefully, over the ensuing years, practices like this started to fade and Bailey's allowed women to work "with the men," and men could try their hand at selling candy.

What was my role in this bustling business? I was hired as a busboy. My job was to wheel a dish cart through the maze of tables and pick up whatever people had decided that they were done with: empty or half-filled hot chocolate mugs, sandwich dishes with scattered crumbs and bits of lettuce, tall curved milkshake glasses with metal holders, and the like. When the cart was full, I would wheel it to the back room where a large, loud, and steamy industrial dishwashing machine was waiting. Once the dishes were washed and dried (all in the same machine), I had to wheel them back out, weaving through the tables and customers, and return the clean dishes to behind the busy lunch counter, where six or seven employees were taking orders, making sandwiches, and scooping ice cream. Often when I had a break, I would grab one of the tiny paper cups that they kept by the water fountain and scoop a tiny amount of ice cream into it followed by a tiny spoonful of hot fudge on the top, for my own little "mini-sundae." It only took a couple of spoonfuls to consume, injecting some sugar energy into me, and then I was back to work.

At one point, on a busy Saturday afternoon, they wanted to try me out at the counter, so I pushed aside the dishcart and began to take customer orders. I loved using the huge old cash register, partly because I got to "do the math." The register didn't add anything up for you: instead, you had to punch in the prices on the rows and columns of big round mechanical buttons and then work out the rest of the details yourself. But it turns out I wasn't ready for the fast-paced order/pay/pickup process of the lunch counter. On my first day behind the counter, I remember this interaction with a customer, who had a long line of waiting customers behind him:

> Customer: *"I'll have a BLT."*
> Me: *"What kind of bread would you like?"*
> Customer: *"White."*
> Me: *"Do you want lettuce and tomato with that?"*
> Customer gives quizzical look...

I was clearly on autopilot, and I don't think I really ate bacon-lettuce-and-tomato sandwiches, so I didn't realize that the lettuce and tomato were an integral part of the BLT experience! Despite the pride that I take today in my intuition, instincts and work ethic, as a teenager, those attributes had yet to develop, a problem that showed up in a few other jobs that I had over the years.

*****

I GOT TO KNOW SOME NEW PEOPLE through the ice cream parlor job, but generally when you're a teenager, friends and acquaintances tend to shift and switch, like birds fluttering around a feeder. Often, your relationships from elementary school weaken or dissolve altogether, especially when friends move away or switch to Catholic or private high schools. As I've mentioned, in Cambridge I was thrown into classes and clubs and lunch periods with kids from other parts of the city that I didn't know well. I eventually became close friends with a lot of new kids, but also casual acquaintances of others for some limited period of time.

At one point, I ended up hanging out regularly with "the two Seans," both of whom were football players at CRLS—one of them lived just a block away from me (I had been friends with his sister since I was little). Although they were both a year younger than me and both football players, for some period of time we found that we had something in common: "tinkering."

We, along with my childhood friend Robbie, wound up going to a massive warehouse in Waltham one day, looking for an old beat-up pinball machine to buy, using money from whatever jobs we had at the time. We found an old machine that we could afford and we brought it to one of the Seans' basement. We played the game for a little while and it was fun to not have to put quarters in to play (we could just open up the coin door and tap the switch inside). But the real project was to take the whole thing completely apart, create a new "playfield," and then put it all back together.

The inside of a pinball machine is even more complex than the public-facing part that has the blinking lights, artwork, bumpers, buttons, and flippers. When we opened it up, it was like we were entering a long room where the floor, ceiling, and all the walls were stuffed with interactivity—wires and solenoids and bolts and screws all jostling for position. We started our overly ambitious project by taking the time to study where everything was and how it was connected. When we were ready, we began to carefully disconnect every one of the many groups of wires from each of the components. As we uncoupled each one, we would put a piece of masking tape on the end of the wire and another on the component it should connect to, labeling each with numbers, starting at "1" (I think we ended up having about 140 of these wires with labels).

Once we had everything apart, we came up with a completely new design for the playfield. Admittedly, I think those guys did more of the design work and construction than I did—I was kind of the electrician and organizer of information. They got a piece of plywood, cut it to the right size and then drilled holes where all the bumpers and other components would be attached. The board was then painted a pleasing shade of high-gloss light blue and reinstalled into the machine. Then it was time to re-connect all the components in their new spots, using the wiring numbers we had established. Amazingly, when we plugged it in and started it up...it worked! Except for one important thing: we could never get the flippers to "flip" with the strength of the original game—and weak flippers make for frustrating play. But it was like a dream to have a pinball machine that no one else did and that we could play any time we wanted.

* * * * *

IN MY SENIOR YEAR, I got another job—this time at a café/deli called The Baigel Bin.[1] It was right outside of Harvard Square on Mass Ave, near the end of Trowbridge Street and just a block from the high school. The place sold bagels, coffee and pastries, and served breakfast and lunch. I worked behind the counter, taking orders and passing them to the chef, making and serving coffee, cutting, toasting, and cream-cheesing the bagels, restocking the supplies, and cleaning up at the end of the day. My friend Glenn also worked there, as did some other kids I vaguely knew from high school. It was a successful and busy place—long lines regularly formed, especially on weekends—although there were hints that it was being financially mismanaged.

Many people smoked cigarettes back in those days, and this included our customers and our workers. The deli provided ashtrays on every table and part of my job was to go around and

1. Yup, they spelled it with that "i" in the middle. I never knew why, but a little 2025 research shows that it is likely related to the original Yiddish spelling of the word.

clean them all out at the end of the day—it must be hard for someone born after this era to imagine sitting at a lunch table with an ashtray filled with cigarette butts! Almost every one of the people who worked at the Baigel Bin would, at some point during the day, announce that they were "going on a cigarette break" and walk away from the counter and stand up against the back wall by the bathroom to light up. It seemed unfair to me that just because I didn't smoke cigarettes, I didn't get a break like they did. I complained about it, but only jokingly. Then one day I announced, "I'm taking a cigarette break," and I borrowed a cigarette and lighter from someone, went over to lean on the wall as the others did, and lit the thing up. Unfortunately, my lungs weren't as enthusiastic about my experiment with tobacco as I was: all I did was start coughing. That would be my first and last cigarette break.

IN MY LAST YEAR AS A HIGH SCHOOL STUDENT, a bunch of friends and I got the idea of organizing a trip to the Bahamas instead of going with the Senior Class on the school's "The Bermuda Trip." I think we wanted to be with friends and not with a bunch of kids we didn't know. We all had jobs to help pay for the flight and hotels and it seemed like an adventurous way to finish up high school. I'd never been on a trip without my parents and certainly didn't know how to organize one. It was an interesting combination of people: me, my closest friend Megan, along with good friends Bobby (the pinball guy), Melina, Carol (the sneak-into-the-new-building girl), Suzie, Aime, and Wati. One of our teachers from CRLS, whom we had become close with, was also with us as sort of our unofficial chaperone, but also a friend (I suspect this kind of arrangement wouldn't happen today).

We spent time at the beach, did some snorkeling, wandered into town, and danced at the disco. I hadn't been a beer-drinker or pot-smoker before my senior year, but had recently started to partake in both (my parents had used the strategy of offering me pot during one of their parties when I was younger—rather than pretend that they never used it— and it worked, because I refused at the time, thinking it made them seem "not themselves"). In the Bahamas, they had vending machines that dispensed cans of beer —how strange! One was filled with cans of Heineken, which I tried, although I've never liked Heineken since—I think it was "skunked."

We also got to know a local Bahamian named Philip who befriended us and sold us a joint or two, which we smoked on the beach. The real excitement was when we went to the casino at the hotel. I decided I would bring just a few dollars with me and try to play roulette. The intricate board and exciting spinning wheel looked like fun. I played for about an hour with someone else from our group and somehow I hit a lucky streak. Amazingly, instead of losing the few dollars I started with, I won about $175 that night, which was quite a bit in 1982.

It was a great trip and we were sad to leave. But on the way back we had a rough flight. I remember trying to board a small plane on the tarmac in the dark of night (maybe to get to the larger airport), but we had to evacuate because of a tropical storm, with heavy rain and strong winds all around us, blowing the palm trees and making them dance. Eventually, we were able to get off the island and head towards Boston, but we first had a layover in New York City. I don't think I'd ever been to New York City before, but because we had a long layover there, we took the subway into the city to explore. At the time, Manhattan was the place you could get things you couldn't find anywhere else—and for prices you wouldn't find anywhere else.

Wati and I walked the streets and eventually found a shop that was selling all kinds of impressive audio equipment, including the *Sony Walkman*, which had recently been introduced to the world. This was the first device that you could hold in the palm of your hand, with headphones on, and walk around listening to a cassette or the radio. I bought a Walkman with my winnings from the roulette table and we were ready to find our way back to the airport and head home to Cambridge to finish our senior year of high school.

One night, about a month later, after hanging around in Harvard Square for hours doing nothing in particular, Wati and I started to walk home. It was past midnight and pretty quiet on the streets. We turned the corner past the Old Burial Ground, where some of those lying in rest had been there since its opening in 1636, and we started walking down Garden Street towards Concord Ave, across from the Cambridge Common. I had my still-new Walkman with me, headphones on, blasting music from a cassette. As we were crossing Appian Way, I went from bouncing to my music to being face-down in the cold street.

It turns out that four or five teenagers had spotted us in Harvard Square and followed us down the street with a plan to rob me of my Walkman. One of the kids took a running leap and, without any warning (I wouldn't have heard much with my headphones on), hit me from behind with his arms around my waist, knocking me to the ground. As the other kids all held Wati, who was yelling at the kid to get off of me, the kid straddled me and grabbed at my Walkman, which was on a clip on my right hip. But I grabbed it too, not wanting to lose my prize possession, and yelled at him to "get the fuck off me!" But I had no leverage to do anything about it. As we struggled over the Walkman, the kid decided he needed to take another approach, so he started punching me in the back of the head over and over again. I still held on, but eventually the punches took their toll and he was able to wrest my Walkman away from me. He got up and they all ran off with their stolen treasure.

I think there was a phone booth across the street, because somehow we called the cops, thinking magically that they would be able to find the kids and get my property back. When they came, my ear was bleeding from a slice into it (the cops said the attacker likely had a knife in his hand, but I didn't think so) but as they took us around the neighborhood in their patrol car, they seemed completely uninterested in what had happened or in finding the kids—they were laughing and talking about something unrelated and didn't even seem to be looking out the window. It dawned on me then that teenagers were not really a priority for the Cambridge Police.

I woke up the next day and had an interesting reflection on race and racism in America. I thought about how a gang of White kids had jumped me in the middle of the night and I doubted that anyone would think that I would now fear any White kid I see walking down the street. But in America, people seem to react whenever they hear of a crime that is committed by a Black or Hispanic person by making a connection with the race of the perpetrator. In other words, if I had reported that a gang of Black kids or Hispanic kids had jumped me and robbed me, there's a reaction that people tend to have that this somehow says something about the nature of Black or Hispanic people. But when it is White kids, there is no generalization that bubbles up in people's minds, even with the same level of violence or lack of compassion for the victim.

When I was growing up, there were White kids that were bullies and there were Black kids that were bullies. There were White kids that were friendly and there were Black kids that were friendly. How do those facts lead to conclusions about one group, but not the other? It's pretty disappointing that in 2025, these generalizations about entire groups of people are not yet considered "old ways of thinking."

AT THIS POINT, my four years of high school were just about up. The place where I hung out, that sometimes fed my interests and sometimes bored me, that taught me some tough but important lessons, that gave me new friends for life, that put me in touch with so many different types of cultures and kids—was going to quickly fade into the background. And I was quite sure of one thing: I had little sense of what would happen next.

*****

I shouldn't end this chapter without saying something about what my parents were doing at this time, because they were leading very busy lives.

My father had long been a member of an interesting group called *Science for the People* (SftP). Since his early years as a geneticist, his focus had always been on both the science and the social responsibility that should come with doing science. Even though my mother wasn't a member of the scientific community, she also worked with SftP for a time, in addition to her English teaching at alternative high schools, leading anti-racist workshops, involvement in unions, and organizing and attending anti-nuke protests.

SftP had come out of the anti-war movement during the Vietnam era. They put out a monthly newsletter with powerful analyses of ethics in science and condemnations of science that reinforced racist, sexist or classist agendas or promoted the corporatization of science. They organized, they protested, and they agitated. Of course, as a kid, I didn't fully grasp what all this meant—but I certainly did notice that my parents were always "going out to meetings" or, more often, having meetings in our living room with a large group of people, making plans and passionately debating issues. On my way out the door to hang out with my friends, I would wave at all these interesting-looking people. I knew generally what the group was about but didn't appreciate the details of their work until much later.

One thing I did notice, in relation to my parents' activities, was the day when our car seemed to have disappeared. *What happened to it?* My parents had donated our car to the Black Panther movement, which had first found a place in Boston in 1968 in the Roxbury neighborhood, after the assassination of Dr. Martin Luther King, Jr. Despite the bad press they often got in the media, the Panthers' activities included providing free breakfast meals, establishing free clinics to those in need (like at the *Franklin Lynch People's Free Health Center* in Roxbury), organizing protests and rallies and marches, and speaking out against police brutality. These activities matched with my parents' values and beliefs about how people should be treated and they felt it was an important self-empowerment movement worthy of support.

As I was getting older, my parents also felt more free to leave me and my brother alone while they had more outdoor adventures, many of them involving bicycling through parts of France or backpacking through the canyons of Utah. My father loved to take photos of desert flowers and my mother enjoyed the wild open spaces and freedom of being out in the wilderness. In my sophomore year, my parents and I went on a bicycling trip in France, biking a total of about 300 miles through the hilly terrain, visiting small villages in the French countryside on rented bikes. Being a teenager, naturally I insisted that I wouldn't go on the trip unless I could bring my tape player with me (it wasn't quite big enough to be called a boom box), so that I could strap it to the back of the bike and listen to my favorite music while we biked through the countryside. I also recall finding pinball machines in pubs in remote parts of France and feeling quite at home with my palms on the machine and fingers on the flipper buttons. We did some camping, ate a lot of French bread and cheese, and took in the sights and smells of the small French villages and huge lavender fields.

In the summers, my parents, my brother Ben, and I would often drive to Pennsylvania to visit my cousins (Tom, Nick, Jennifer, Adam, Dana) and aunts and uncles (Linda, Peter, Joanne, David) on my mother's side, who lived in the mountainous and remote small town of Henryville. I dreaded the five-hour drive, but playing MadLibs or "the license plate game" at least kept me from losing my mind before we arrived. I will say, though, that the experience of "going out to the country" was always worth it, with lots of cousins (there were a bunch of second cousins and other relatives who were also there) and cookouts and softball games and swimming in the lake and taking shortcuts through the mysterious woods.

I was a bit closer to my father's side of the family because they all lived locally—especially the ones that lived in Cambridge, not far from Porter Square, as opposed to the ones that lived in Framingham. We would get together with aunt Gail and uncle Mike and their kids Dan and Kathe to go to movies in Harvard Square or for meals at Thanksgiving or at Christmas time (where cousins Jim and Jen and their parents Pepi and Harvey would join us). To be clear, this side of my family had Jewish ancestry, but none were religious and we "went along" with the American gift-giving Christmas traditions.

We also spent a good amount of time together in the summer at a house in Mashpee, on Cape Cod. It was a house that in the 1970s was surrounded by a lot of overgrown wilderness around it and had a dirt road nearby that led to Wakeby Lake, where we would catch minnows, take a dip, and drift lazily around on a rowboat. There were very few houses there at the time and no stores to speak of. In the 1990s, long after we stopped going there in the summers, it started to grow rapidly. I shudder to think of the thousands of trees that have been taken down since then to make way for the flood of new developments and strip malls that have cropped up in the years since then.

Working at the Baigel Bin, around 1981. The cook, Al, is on the far right

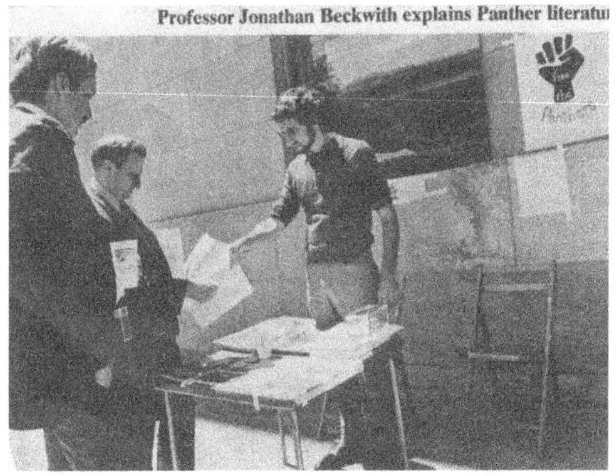

My father passing out Black Panther literature in the early 1970s

7

NOW WHAT?

"P*ut a glide in your stride, a dip in your hip, and come on to the Mothership.*"

THESE ARE THE WORDS I had printed below my senior yearbook photo in 1982. Some kids might have chosen a phrase that they were known for using (one kid had "So I says to myself: self, I says..."), others might have chosen a quote that reflected on their future after high school. *So what was I trying to say with my choice*? The words were not my own, but were lyrics from one of my favorite albums at the time.

George Clinton, as the front man of the group Parliament, sang/spoke the "dip in your hip" lyrics in the 1975 song *Mothership Connection*, from the album of the same name. The lyrics didn't have much of a message, but the bass and drums, the horns and the singing, the surprising chord and tempo and style changes—to me, they all created a piece of artwork, six minutes and fourteen seconds long, that I could listen to over and over. I loved the way the "glide in your stride" phrase sounded and wanted it to be right there with me in the yearbook. Looking back, my choice showed a love of that music, but also might have been a reflection of the fact that I had no real plan for my life, other than to listen to music, be with friends, and wait and see what happens next.

*****

EARLY IN THE WINTER OF 1981, I began to apply to colleges, simply because it was what appeared to be "next" in life. I was going to attend college *not* because I had a vision of what I wanted to do with my life or a passion that I wanted to follow or an understanding of what the college experience was and wanted to be part of it—none of those things were true. If both of my parents hadn't attended college, I might even have considered doing something different after high school. And because I was applying to colleges for the wrong reasons, it was going to turn out to be a bumpy ride. But that ride also led me to some of the most impactful (and positive) decisions I would make in my life.

I applied to six colleges (Brown, Cornell, UPenn, UMass/Amherst, the University of Michigan/Ann Arbor, and Carnegie Mellon). In the late winter of 1982, I heard back from each of them. I had been rejected by the first three (the more competitive liberal arts schools on my list) and accepted by the last three. The rejections were likely because, while I was a pretty good student in high school, I didn't tend to "stand out in the crowd." I was excited about Math and Computer Science, but many CRLS students were more capable than me in those areas. The only clubs or organizations I joined were the Math and Computer Science Teams. I also didn't play organized sports and didn't belong to any civic organizations. I was a pretty good writer, had an interest in politics and world events, and I followed the news by reading The Boston Globe—but of course, the colleges didn't know about that.

I was capable enough as a student to know how to get decent grades in my classes and spent plenty of time writing computer programs, but I didn't have a plan for what I would do in college and didn't even understand what college was. And I don't think I cared: I liked my life in Cambridge, listening to music and hanging with friends.

I didn't know how to decide between the three colleges that accepted me. I did realize that committing to Carnegie-Mellon would probably mean committing to computer science or robotics as a career and I must have been unsure enough about what I wanted to do with my life that making that commitment felt like too big of a leap. In the end, I decided to attend the University of Michigan at Ann Arbor—a good school, but for a variety of reasons, not the right one for me at that point in my life.

Looking back, only now has it dawned on me that Carnegie-Mellon must have appreciated the work I did in high school math and computer science, given that C-M was one of the top schools for computer science in the country and, even today, shows up second in the rankings, behind only MIT. But at that point in my life, although I had competency and I had interest, I didn't have a goal in mind. I had no ambition that was driving me. And perhaps I was a bit scared of not being successful at a "big time" school like Carnegie-Mellon. But, as it turns out, Michigan wasn't the solution either.

THE UNIVERSITY OF MICHIGAN at Ann Arbor educates approximately 50,000 students each year. The sheer size of the population made it easy for an academically directionless student like myself to get lost in the shuffle. Most of the students there had grown up in the Midwest (at least that's what it felt like to me when I moved into my dorm). I was so used to New England—and more specifically Cambridge—that I had a hard time relating to the midwestern college kids I met, who I thought had strange accents, listened to different music, and seemed like they existed in a different culture from mine. Ann Arbor was a cool city (they had a pinball arcade!), but that wasn't going to help me get focused. The dorm was also miles away from campus and required a shuttle bus just to get to class. In the end, I just couldn't find my place within the University of Michigan (although I did at one point try to pursue my passion for music by becoming an early-morning music DJ on the school's AM station).

I'm not proud to admit that I flunked out after one semester. I played pinball, smoked pot with my roommate (who years later became born again and had nine children), listened to music, and often skipped classes (although when I was in class, I was focused and interested). In other words, I sabotaged myself. I could have succeeded in the courses I had signed up for, but something about me wouldn't let that happen. I basically got the four worst grades you can get: in one course, I received an *I* (incomplete), in another a *W* (withdraw), in the third, a *D-* (yeah, that's a passing grade, but not really), and lastly, an *F*. When the semester ended, U. of M. simply stamped "DNR" on my transcript, meaning "Do Not Return." They knew what was up—and so did I.

ONCE I WAS BACK HOME, it was clear I wasn't going back to college right away. But I did have some useful skills. For one, I was pretty good at writing computer programs. *Could I get a job doing this?* Well, being a college dropout probably wasn't going to help. In the end, my father came to the rescue. I know that makes me kind of lucky, but I also know that a lot of people land jobs through knowing someone who knows someone, or by joining the family business. In this case, my father ran a microbiology lab at Harvard Medical School in Boston near the Fenway and they needed someone who knew something about computers. I was hired to write programs for the lab (those programs were in BASIC because the only computer they had in the lab in 1983 was the newly-released *Rainbow 100* by DEC and it had a BASIC interpreter installed already).

The most complex program—the one that I spent many

weeks writing—was one that would help organize information about gene sequences into a database and then provide an analysis of each sequence. It took in all the data for a sequence (made up of the bases, A, T, C, G) and then calculated and displayed a graphic showing the degrees of hydrophobicity (where it repelled water) or hydrophilicity (where it was attracted to water) of the entire sequence. This meant that in my display, there was a central line down the middle and each A, T, C, or G was some distance to the left of that line (hydrophobic) or to the right (hydrophilic), rendering visual something that was previously only represented by masses of data. Once it was up and running, researchers could enter any sequence and quickly get a long printout of this analysis for that sequence.

I also assisted one of my father's postdocs with her research in the lab. Sometimes I just cleaned pipettes and flasks, but I also learned a bit about growing cultures on a petri dish and using a centrifuge. I definitely wasn't as good a lab assistant as I was a programmer, given that my high school biology and chemistry skills were pretty weak. But I did what I could and I was probably seen as helpful to the people doing research in the lab. What I really loved was writing programs and getting them to accomplish the given task. This was a temporary job and I would look for other work when summer came, but it turned out to be a great way to establish a routine and feel productive and useful, as opposed to sliding into whatever the world of an unemployed college dropout would have felt like.

*****

WHEN I HAD LEFT for college the previous fall, my friends had themselves also headed off to other parts of the country. My pinball buddy Bobby and my friend Wati both went to school in California. Megan, my good friend and Appleton Road neighbor, headed to New York City. Maria went north to Maine, while Melina and Paul both stayed in Massachusetts.

I also had several friends who did not apply to college after high school at all. For some, it just wasn't part of the tradition of their family—perhaps neither of their parents had attended college. These friends probably didn't see a need for college in their lives. Maybe that was because they already had skills they could use to get good jobs or because they couldn't picture themselves being a student and taking classes for another four years—most likely, it was both. Because I had a lot of friends in this situation, when I moved back home that winter from Michigan, I didn't feel at all alone in Cambridge.

During that winter and the coming spring, I began spending more time with friends I had become closer to at the end of high school and over the previous summer, especially Glenn, Carol, Brian, and Conrad. That spring, Glenn and I both got our motorcycle licenses (I still didn't have an automobile driver's license) and we bought a motorcycle together: a fun, but small, Kawasaki Bushmaster 90 (later we also bought the larger Kawasaki Z200 together). When I wasn't riding my bicycle or taking the shuttle bus from Harvard Square to the lab, I would take the Bushmaster, riding along the Charles River on Storrow Drive and getting off at Kenmore to head to the Longwood Medical area.

I spent a lot of time hanging out with this crew, including Glenn and Conrad's brother Karl and their friend Tom. We'd sit around and "shoot the shit," looking for things to do, like playing an early video console game[1] for hours at a time. Someone would head out to get another six-pack of beer every now and then, but we otherwise had a lot of fun just hanging out for hours, playing the game, talking, and laughing. We also worked on cars and motorcycles on the street (changing the starter or replacing brake pads), went for rides on our bikes to Walden Pond, and hung out at other friends' houses, or in Harvard Square.[2] We also regularly

1. The game was *Archon*, which came out in 1983 and was one of the very first video games put out by EA (Electronic Arts).

2. When I was younger, there was no "Pit" in Harvard Square, but we would hang

went out to see bands at clubs like The Channel in Boston and the Western Front in Cambridge. But the thing that had a major impact on my life at this time was actually what went on in the basement of a two-family home on Ivy Street in Cambridge, starting in early 1983.

The Route to Roots

THAT BASEMENT WAS IN THE HOME of Glenn and Conrad's mother, Ilene, and was typical of most basements back then: dusty, with cobwebs, populated with boilers, water heaters, cardboard boxes for storage, wood sash windows, and iron posts holding up house-bearing wooden beams. But the reason I spent time in that basement was for the musical jam sessions that happened down there.

Brian and Conrad had started playing music several years earlier, finding their spiritual energy fueled by the sounds of reggae music and by the brotherhood found with the Jamaican and Caribbean population of Cambridge that they had gotten to know. Brian, in particular, had grown up near the Central Square area, where a large number of Caribbean immigrant families lived, and with whom he had made deep connections. He would spend hours learning bass lines and playing drums with some of the interesting characters he'd met around his neighborhood.

I wasn't a musician at the time—my parents had set me up with piano and drum lessons when I was younger, but my resistance to things outside my main interests got in the way and I gave up on both quickly. But as I headed down the stairs to that basement, I was now hearing great-sounding *live* music. The music was being channeled through people, through their instru-

---

out near its future location and at small parks or at the Mug 'n' Muffin. When the MBTA finished their new subway station around 1983, part of the result was a new place to hang out, which was known as "The Pit" because it started its life as a construction hole and later became a sunken brick plaza right next to the subway entrance.

ments and voices, and I could feel the shared passion they had for the music. I took in the deep sound of the drum and bass, the chick-a-chick of the guitar, the smooth organ sounds, and the rich voices of the singers. There was a mix of Black and White and Caribbean and American musicians and singers, all synchronized with each other.[3]

Horace, who was on drums and vocals, was from Jamaica and had come to Cambridge when he was young and attended high school in Cambridge a couple of years before me (he also had been a founding member of one of the first reggae bands in the Boston area: The I-Tones). Conrad played bass lines that were deep and solid as a rock. Brian would also play bass and was a dynamic drummer and a burgeoning singer. Iman played the keyboards and sang lead vocals—he hailed from Barbados. Glenn would sometimes play the "skank" on his black Gibson guitar. The lead singer Rocky (from some Caribbean island, I lost track) had one of the smoothest voices I'd ever heard. Inando played percussion and was a dynamic singer when he was on stage—he was from Barbados (Rocky and Inando had both been lead singers with the great band *Healin' of the Nations*). Fleur was a Jamaican singer, dub poet, and percussion player with a rich voice. Sometimes Tom—an old friend of Conrad and Glenn's from Lexington —would sing or play harmonica and sometimes a different Tom would play drums. There was even a saxophone player who showed up at different points.

How did all these people connect and end up together in Conrad's basement? It wasn't until years later that I understood the many connections that Brian had to a wide variety of local musicians, singers, DJs, deejays (one spins records, the other chants on the mic), and other characters from the reggae scene.

I had always loved reggae, having listened to that section of

3. Much of what went on in the basement were jam sessions, but this crew also did a couple of gigs and so were practicing songs for the live shows - they performed as the band "Radication."

my parents' record collection over and over when I was younger and later starting to build a small collection of my own with UB40, Mikey Dread, Bob Marley, Steel Pulse and others. Still, up to this point, my tastes had been evenly spread across reggae, funk, jazz, ska and new wave music, with reggae being just one branch of my personal musical tree. My childhood friend Paul—whom I had been friends with since he found a seat for me on the first day of sixth grade—was Jamaican, but he had more interest in American funk, pop, and rock than reggae and so our friendship had never pushed me in that direction. But once I started listening to the likes of "roots reggae" artists like Burning Spear, Prince Far I, Ini Kamoze, the Mighty Diamonds, Gregory Isaacs, the Abyssinians, the Itals, and the Meditations, I came to an understanding that reggae music was not just "another kind of music"—it was multifaceted and it was meaningful.

Reggae is a kind of folk music, a music from the people; a type of gospel music, heavily spiritual; a protest music, fiercely fighting against injustice; and a uniquely Jamaican form of expression, coming from a place with a complicated history of slavery, immigration and indentured servitude, fights for independence, natural beauty, and proud and strong connections to African cultural and musical traditions. Reggae music not only had the tempo, sound, and texture that resonated musically with me, but it also spoke directly to some of the values that I held.

As spring turned to summer and I became exposed to more of the local reggae scene up close and personal, I bought an electronic keyboard.[4] It was a big heavy *Crumar Orchestrator*, which had rudimentary piano, brass, synth, and string sounds, but also —most importantly—a killer deep bass sound that was perfect for reggae. It wasn't long before I could play any chords I needed to and was figuring out bass lines from some of my favorite songs

4. I got the keyboard by calling a number found in the *For Sale* section of the Boston Globe. Back in those days, you could go to a used instrument shop or you could look in the paper to find something like this. That was pretty much it.

—and I learned to hold the bass line steady on my left hand while playing the skank chords on my right hand.

I wasn't the greatest musician, but I think I felt something that a lot of traditionally-trained non-reggae musicians had some trouble acquiring: an internal sense of how Jamaican reggae music should sound. The rhythm and timing of reggae "flips the script" on the Western modern tradition of rock, R&B, and even jazz. I've seen and heard some professional musicians try to play reggae, but fail: they end up drifting to playing the rhythm on the "1 and 3" instead of the "2 and 4." Or if they get that right, they misunderstand the role of their instrument in making the music.

Reggae is based on a heavy, solid, and steady drum and bass, with most of the other instruments there to support that foundation, rarely taking the spotlight as lead instruments. Since I was learning to play music solely for the purpose of playing reggae, my musical foundation was aligned with reggae's from the start and I wasn't hampered by being trained in any Western tradition.

Once I was exposed to this music live, it became something that I felt deeply and wanted to experience as much as possible. You know those moments in your life when you need to hear some music to make you feel better, or to relax to, or to dance to? For me, those moments have centered on reggae music for almost 40 years now. Despite being a white American, this was the music that not only resonated with me the most, but also inspired me to do whatever I could to become part of creating it and experiencing it through the sounds, the history, and the people connected with it.

*****

SUMMER WAS RAPIDLY APPROACHING. This meant that friends from high school who had been at college were now returning to Cambridge from different parts of the country.

My friend Megan had been at Barnard College in New York City, where she had found herself in the same English class as a girl named Cori, who was from the Bay Area in California. They first noticed each other's colored streaks in their hair and when they got to know each other better, they found they shared a love of alternative music styles, a sharp wit, and a rejection of many societal norms. Cori and Megan quickly became close friends. So when the end of the semester came, instead of Cori going back to California for the summer, they came up with a plan for her to stay at Megan's house in Cambridge. Of course, I lived right across the street from Megan's house, so I met Cori shortly after her arrival[5]. I found that she had a relaxed vibe about her; she did wild things with her hair, like shaving it all off or coloring it pink or blue; she owned a skateboard; she was smart; and she was cute as a button.

That summer, in addition to my musical friends, I hung out with Cori and Megan, listening to music, playing games, talking, and visiting other friends. Eventually, Cori and I became closer. And closer. We started dating and she soon became the most serious girlfriend that I'd ever had. More than dating, we were falling in love (as much as any pair of 19-year-olds can know that). We began to spend almost all of our non-working hours together, going out to shows, visiting friends, going on motorcycle rides, our two lives melting into one. (In addition to working and spending my free time with Cori, I also started taking courses at Harvard Extension School. Over three semesters, I would take a math course, a French course, and later an analog and digital electronics course.)

Cori found work at Paco's Tacos (Glenn also worked there) in Harvard Square, across the street from the Galleria Cinema. My work at the lab was wrapping up, so I got a job at a local fruit and vegetable store, *Le Jardin*, which was right around the corner from my house. Megan had worked there before me and probably helped me get the job. I mostly did grunt work like stocking the

---

5. Actually, I officially first met Cori briefly the previous November, when she spent Thanksgiving with Megan in Cambridge

shelves, moving boxes, and mopping and cleaning up. I wasn't all that great at it because I didn't know fruits and vegetables that well—if I was told to get a box of arugula or scallions, I would have to ask what that was.

*****

IT WAS A FRIDAY NIGHT and I guess we had nothing else to do. At this point in our lives, a weekend night was an empty slate, a free spot on the board, waiting for a piece to be plopped down onto it; anything could happen. But on this night, the best we could come up with was to just go for a motorcycle ride (me on the Bushmaster, Glenn and Carol on the Z200; Cori was at work). It was late summer and it was warm and the evening felt worthy of a ride.

We didn't have a destination, but that didn't matter: we headed out of Cambridge towards Belmont, taking a turn onto Trapelo Road (which, if you keep going for another 12 miles, would take you all the way to Walden Pond). We had nothing specific in mind, but we were ready for anything...or were we? Actually, at this point Glenn only had a motorcycle learner's permit and didn't have a license plate, instead settling for a cardboard spoof of his plate with the numbers drawn onto it. This would all be fine as long as we "stayed out of trouble." But, of course, trouble sometimes finds you.

As we rode towards the crest of the hill, enjoying the wind on our faces, Glenn noticed that there was a cop car behind us. Glenn called out to me to pull up and ride directly behind him to try to block the view of his missing license plate so the cop wouldn't notice and would pass us by without incident. The way Glenn tells it, I did not do my job correctly (since I can't recall, I'll take his word for it). The cop pulled all three of us over and sat us down on the curb in the warm night. He pretty quickly determined that Glenn's bike was unlicensed and that he was illegally transporting a passenger at night, with only a learner's permit. This was not good. It meant that the Z200 would have to be impounded and that our summer night adventure was suddenly over.

Because of the particular infractions, Glenn had to be taken to the station that night and even put in a cell for a time. I couldn't take Carol with me on the Bushmaster because it didn't handle a passenger well—especially on the hills of Belmont—so Carol's boyfriend Donny had to pick her up. They also bailed Glenn out after he'd spent a couple of hours at the Belmont Police station.

What happened with the motorcycle?

Between the fines and the daily storage fees, we couldn't afford to get the Z200 back from the towing company, and so, who knows? Maybe it's still sitting in a City of Cambridge lot somewhere gathering dust, waiting to be picked up four decades later.

WITH SEPTEMBER RAPIDLY APPROACHING, I was not looking forward to Cori going back to school 250 miles away in Manhattan. I could visit her in New York, but our relationship felt so powerful and at the same time was still so young—it didn't feel like it was ready to be cut off this way. After a lot of consideration, Cori made a big decision: she would put off returning to Barnard until the spring semester and would stay living in Cambridge and find a job. We both wanted to continue to be together and I was overjoyed at her decision.

In the fall, it was now Cori's turn to find work at *Le Jardin.* She was very good with plants and so was perfect for working with the florists they had on staff there.

My friends who were going to college left town once again, leaving Cori and I to spend even more time together than we had before. We also hung out with Glenn, Carol, Donny, and Conrad, playing cards, drinking, going out to shows. But there was another decision looming, that couldn't be avoided: what would Cori do in the spring? We both knew what the right thing to do was: Cori should return to Barnard for the 1984 spring semester and continue her studies (she planned to be an astronomy major).

That winter, Cori packed up her stuff and she returned to New York. We agreed that we would call and write to each other and visit as much as possible. We were in fact able to do all of those things, although it was harder for her as a student to leave New York City in the middle of a semester, so more often I would take the bus from Boston to New York.

This worked for a while, but has an arrangement like this ever lasted long? We tried for as long as we could, but we were living in different cities and completely different environments and before long it was over, despite very strong feelings between us. Cori was the one who recognized that it wasn't going to work and I had a very hard time accepting that, but eventually I had no choice but to try to "move on."

It was also time for *me* to consider going back to school. If I started the next fall, I would have taken a full year and a half off from pursuing a college education. I applied to Tufts in Medford and reapplied to UMass/Amherst. By the spring of 1984, I had gotten my acceptance letter from UMass and planned to attend in the fall. It was time to "start over again."

There was one last event for me that spring: I traveled to Jamaica for the first time with Megan's father Jeff, for a week. Through his Boston Globe connections, he had made arrangements to stay with a family that lived and worked in Negril—the Williamses. It was great hearing reggae music everywhere I went—on the mini-buses we used to get around, blaring out of local homes and bars and restaurants, even in the airport. The beaches were beautiful and Alvin Williams took us up into the hills where he grew his vegetables and his ganja. I met a lot of people and got an on-the-ground feel for the culture. Yet I struggled with the concept of being a middle-class American coming to an "island playground." I was glad I wasn't staying at some walled-off resort, but I still couldn't quite shake the feeling, given the poverty that existed there.

*****

A MAJOR CHANGE WAS COMING to my life in the fall, but I continued to play music, work, and take courses in that summer of 1984. The last course I would take at Harvard Extension School was *Digital and Analog Electronics*, which met in the Harvard Science Center, not far from CRLS. Two experiences from taking that interesting course ended up having a lasting impact on me.

First, the content of the course was infamous for being very challenging, but also contained some of the most fascinating concepts I had ever learned about—ones that would stay with me and I would eventually apply as a teacher myself many years later. We first learned about analog electronics, which is sort of the stuff you would find in any old radio or stereo component, connected to each other by wires: resistors, capacitors, inductors, transistors, and diodes. We learned about the properties of each and the ways they can be combined in a circuit to affect the signals that pass through them (we built and tested many of the circuits we studied). The analog portion of the course was building a foundational understanding of the components that in fact had led to the entire field of digital electronics.

In the digital electronics part of the course, things became more complex. Digital electronics is mostly about understanding microchips—things like op-amps, multiplexers and demultiplexers, logic gates, registers, decoders and encoders, timers, RAM, ROM, and CPUs. We also studied the underlying theory and mathematics behind how all of these things worked in combination. The final project was to design and build, based on all the theory we had learned, a working microcomputer. The entire production was built on a breadboard (a platform for building temporary circuits without soldering). We wired the CPU to the RAM and to other microchips, seven-segment displays, and little toggle switches. We tested it out with various tasks and while it wasn't perfect, it still represented a physical manifestation of the power of combining electronics and design with mathematics and logic. The knowledge I got from this course influenced my education at UMass/Amherst and was part of what I was able to pass on to my own students many years later when I began teaching high school computer science.

The second thing that came out of taking that course was the connection I made with my lab partner, James. He was ten to fifteen years older than me, but we connected immediately and had a great time together, struggling through this demanding course. I got to know him better when he would sometimes give me a ride home on his way to Watertown after class. James was a musician who played saxophone, flute, piano, standup bass, and many other instruments. His "day job" was working with electronics, repairing heart monitors, so this class was very helpful to him, also. When the course came to an end, we stayed in touch, hanging out a lot and eventually playing music together live and in the recording studio—he even played at my wedding! But let's not get ahead of ourselves...

The first day in my University of Michigan dorm room

8

LET'S TRY THIS AGAIN

WOULD IT WORK THIS TIME? I was two years older and presumably more mature. I'd taken college courses and gotten excited about them. I certainly *should* have been ready to take more seriously the kinds of educational opportunities that I'd previously squandered.

In September of 1984, I moved my belongings into room 307 in the Baker dormitory in Central Campus at the University of Massachusetts in Amherst, about an hour and a half drive from Cambridge. It was time to start college—again. The room was typical of dorms at that time: small, with a couple of outlets, a couple of closets, a couple of bookshelves, a couple of bunk beds for the bodies that would reside there, and a single big window that looked out on the rest of the campus. It was the "perfect place" to put two strangers together and see what would happen.

But I have absolutely no memory of my first roommate's name. Or what he looked like. There are only three things I do recall about him: he was a lacrosse player; he really wanted to live in "the towers" in Southwest, not in our relatively quiet low-rise dorm; and he kept a funnel in his closet, which he would fill up with as much beer as possible, put the tube in his mouth, then let go and chug away.

The reason I can't recall much else about him is that three weeks after we moved in, John Doe got his wish: he was off to Southwest, taking his funnel and his lacrosse stick with him. I don't know how my first year back in college would have played out if I had been stuck in a room with that guy, but I suspect it would not have been joyful.

Once my roommate was gone and I had my stereo set up, I would blast music through the speakers while I was doing Calculus problems or writing an English paper or whatever else I might have been working on. One day (I think within days of J. Doe moving out), while playing the 12" single *Don't Fake the Funk*[1] on my turntable—and with my head buried in my books—two girls/young women danced right into my room, moving perfectly with the beat. I had no idea who they were, but I could tell they had good taste in music and so I rolled with it.

Joni and Monica had been good friends in their hometown of Norwood, Massachusetts, and had just started at UMass. They would be my first new friends at UMass and would come by often to listen to music and hang out. In the coming years, we would continue to hang out and go see music together or talk late into the night about culture and spirituality and politics.

That other bed in my room was empty for only a week or so before I got a new roommate: Artie, from Plainville, Massachusetts. We shared musical and political and cultural interests and we got along great. While I was going to class and studying and exploring Amherst and the college campus, I was also getting to know some of Artie's friends and others in the dorm. Artie was a big fan of the Grateful Dead (I think he'd call himself a "Deadhead"), as were a lot of his friends. I knew almost nothing about the Dead other than hearing the song *Truckin'* on the radio when it became popular. I certainly didn't know anything about a

1. *Don't Fake the Funk* was recorded by the great, but little-known, Boston funk band Prince Charles and the City Street Band.

massive subculture of people that followed this band around the country. I think this was due to geography.

It seemed like a lot of the Deadheads I met were from rural or suburban towns, whereas most of the people I knew in the city were fans of R&B, funk, disco, reggae, rock, or punk bands. I was certainly intrigued by my new friends' fascination with this scene and eventually Artie and some others got me to go to a Dead concert in Springfield, Massachusetts, at the Civic Center. I had a little fun, but it became clear to me that this music and this scene (including the LSD and magic mushrooms a lot of people seemed to be taking) were not for me. I couldn't relate to the musical or singing style, or to the lyrics. I could understand how other people would flock to it, but it wasn't my style. I did, however, share similar viewpoints with a lot of the people I met who were into the Dead. The sense of spirituality, the anti-capitalism and the anti-war aesthetic resonated with a lot of the reasons that I was so into reggae music.

Making the Adjustment

WHY WAS I A MATH MAJOR? As you can probably tell from the earlier part of my life, I didn't have a "*This is what I want to do with my life*" and so all that was left for me was a "*This is what I'm good at.*" I didn't think I was going to become a musician or a writer or a programmer or a teacher or anything specific, really. I certainly wasn't thinking that I would "be a mathematician" after college. I had to pick a major and I thought I could pull this one off, so I went for it.

That first semester, I found myself working pretty hard in my classes, sometimes helping other students in study groups. I met a lot of new people and started to DJ some parties on campus. In the dorm, I sometimes joined people in the common space on the first floor for musical performances or to gather around the TV to watch the NBA playoffs or the latest episode of *Cheers* on Thursday nights, which was always fun. I sometimes went home for the weekend to visit friends still living in Cambridge (a Peter Pan bus ran between Boston and Northampton). This was one of the downsides of going to school in Massachusetts: it was a little too easy to make the trip to Cambridge and hang out with old friends, rather than fully dedicate myself to a new life in Amherst.

Through Artie and the Deadhead crew, I eventually met Sue, who was a UMass student from Pittsfield, Massachusetts, near the western border with New York State. She was a very caring person and had the sweetest smile, the greatest laugh, and the cutest voice. By March of 1985, we had begun a romance, which helped me try to put Cori out of my mind for a while (easier said than done). In a way, Sue and I were very different from each other, but I think that made for a fun relationship. We spent a lot of time together and I remember one late night taking a long walk with her, holding hands. As we approached the parking lot in the back of a building, I started humming some gentle music to her and we stopped walking. With no one else around, we slow-danced to my imaginary song, surrounding each other and feeling the world melting away. I was generally a pretty shy person when it came to dating and starting relationships, but once I "fell in love," I tended to be a romantic person.

As far as school was concerned, I was doing pretty well. Not always, though. The title I gave to my first paper for my College English course in the second semester was "Procrastination." The reason for that title was that I *started* writing the paper after it was already due and then turned it in a full two weeks late. It was very well-written and I got an A+ on the paper, but then I lost more than a full grade for lateness. I knew that I still hadn't completely figured out how to attain (and keep) my focus on getting school work done, which was the thing that got me kicked out of Michigan and still haunted me to some degree in my Harvard Extension School courses.

But over my four years, I had some interesting and inspiring professors teaching some fascinating courses at UMass that I thoroughly enjoyed. I was a math major, so I had many interesting and truly challenging math courses, but since the details of those are a bit too technical to go into here, I will focus on what else I got academically out of my four years there.

Definitely a Liberal Arts Education

IN MY FRESHMAN YEAR, other than the writing class I've mentioned, I really enjoyed two computer science classes that I took. One was based on Pascal, one of the top programming languages back then. The other was a course in Assembly Language programming—the type of programming that is done more at the "chip level" than through an operating system. Those courses involved many late nights trying to get code to work before the deadline, but the problem-solving and reward-based nature of programming, along with my fascination with complexity, was something I yearned for and that continued to energize me.

I also took a great course in the Comparative Literature department called *Brave New Worlds*, which was taught by a saxophone-playing, pink-convertible-driving professor. We read ten books or so, each with either a utopian or a dystopian theme. They included *The Fate of the Earth* by Jonathan Schell, *Woman on the Edge of Time* by Marge Piercy, *Brave New World* by Aldous Huxley, *1984* by George Orwell, *Herland* by Charlotte Perkins Gilman, and others. The papers all involved comparing two or more of the books with each other, which was an interesting challenge. I got a lot out of that class, did more writing than I had ever done, and really enjoyed the discussions.

In my sophomore year, I took a course in the Afro-American Studies department called The Harlem Renaissance, learning all about the musicians, the writers, the poets, the playwrights, the actors, and the artists that flourished throughout the 1920s and 1930s in Harlem. I loved every minute of it. We even learned about a great poet (Claude McKay) who had emigrated from Jamaica and who wrote a lot of his poetry in 1920s Jamaican dialect. Jacob Lawrence was my favorite painter from this period. The course also led me to later read *Black Like Me* by John Howard Griffin, *Invisible Man* by Ralph Ellison, *The Autobiography of Malcolm X* by Alex Haley, and *Soul On Ice* by Eldridge Cleaver (remember when I said I only read comic books and not books? That had clearly changed).

That same year, I took two courses in the Electrical Engineering department that I got really into, both on *Digital and Computer Systems.* The concepts I learned in that Harvard Extension School course I had taken gave me a great foundation for these courses, but I learned so much more about digital electronics, logic gates, microchips, and complex circuit design approaches.

In my junior year, I took another Afro-American Studies course: *The Evolution of Apartheid.* This was about four years before apartheid in South Africa collapsed under the weight of worldwide protests and Nelson Mandela's bravery. The course was supposed to be taught by the Jamaican author and civil rights activist Michael Thelwell, but I think something pulled him away from it at some point and a graduate student of his finished the course with us. Thelwell had actually founded that department in the 1970s after getting his master's at UMass in 1969. It was his activism in the 1980s that led to a change in U.S. tax law relating to U.S. companies doing business in South Africa.

That year, I also signed up for a course called *Modern Logic Design*. This would be the third course I would take in the Electrical Engineering department, but in it, I had finally met my match. I was often the only non-engineering major in these courses, but still, I reveled in the learning in those first two courses and felt proud of how well I could do in them. However, I could no longer keep up with students who were doing engineering full-time. Even though I found the topic fascinating, I withdrew from the class once I started feeling completely lost and out of my league.

In my senior year, in addition to my most challenging math

courses, I took a great sociology course about China, an anthropology course called *North American Indians*, and a course called *The History of Jazz* in the music department, where we learned about the history of the development of jazz, but also about the different musicians and the development of the different styles over the decades. I still recall learning about the concept of "vocalese," which is when a jazz singer takes a purely instrumental jazz piece and then creates lyrics that are sung to the melody of the main lead instrument. One great example would be Dizzy Gillespie's song *Night In Tunisia*, which he wrote in 1942. Dizzy played a complex and beautiful lead trumpet in that song, which any jazz aficionado is very familiar with. Over the years after it came out, several different artists wrote and then sang lyrics to match exactly with the notes he played in his lead, including Sarah Vaughan, the Manhattan Transfer, and my favorite: Chaka Khan. If you know the opening melody to the song, you can imagine Chaka Khan singing these words right alongside Dizzy's trumpet solo:

> *"A long-time-ago...in the '40s*
> *Dizzy-and-Bird...gave us this song*
> *They-called-it-A-Night...in Tunisia...*
> *and the melody still lingers on..."*

I also took, on a whim, a T'ai Chi course during my senior year. This had a lasting impact on my life (like many other experiences during these years). It led me to better health, to a calmer mind, and later to exploring the Tao Te Ching and to on-and-off practice of both yoga and T'ai Chi for decades.

I want to be clear about one thing, though: I did not suddenly become a super-responsible A student at UMass. My grades were mixed. I contributed to my classes and I was engaged and excited about what I was learning, but that didn't always translate into following through by doing my assigned work or getting it done on time. I would sometimes prefer to play pinball in the Student

Union or frisbee on the lawn or to party with roommates, rather than getting to the work I knew I could do, but was avoiding. I wish I could explain my procrastinating mind at the time—a trait which is pretty much the exact opposite of who I would later become—but it's not something I really understand well, even to this day.

My academic experience at UMass was just one aspect of my college experience. The rest of my life—the social part—was of course progressing alongside the academic part on its own parallel track, with all the twists and turns of a good rollercoaster, including the flat, calm parts and the slow, rickety climbs to the top of each peak.

* * * * *

THE SUMMER AFTER my freshman year, I bought my first car. I got it for $50 from my musician friend James: a well-worn Chrysler Town & Country station wagon, the kind with the fake wood panels on the side. It got terrible gas mileage and I had to always carry a screwdriver with me in case I needed to prop open the air feed to the carburetor to get it started—but the freedom it gave me was priceless. I certainly couldn't move my stuff back to Amherst in the fall on a motorcycle! Also, at one point that same summer, Sue made the long trip from Western Massachusetts to Cambridge to visit so that we could spend time together. She met a lot of my friends from Cambridge and I later visited her out in Pittsfield.

When I returned to UMass for my sophomore year, I was able to apply to get out of the rule that freshmen and sophomores were required to live in the dorms and I moved into an apartment in one of those cheap student housing developments outside of Amherst—this one was called Rolling Green. My roommates were two guys who had grown up in Cambridge, but I hadn't known them well. (The next two years, I also lived in apartments: first in a rundown row house in the nearby city of Northampton in my junior year with one roommate, and then with two roommates in the upstairs of an Amherst two-family home in my senior year.)

Now that we were both back in Amherst, I had assumed that Sue and I would pick right up where we left off. But instead, I was in for a bit of surprise. In the first week of school, Sue told me she needed to be alone and that she was basically breaking up with me, but still wanted to hang out. It was the classic "let's be friends" talk. I was surprised, but tried not to let it show and so I "played it cool." But I didn't know what to think or why it was happening. Within the next few weeks, it started to seem like she didn't even want to hang out.

At some point, a few weeks later, I saw her on campus with a guy and found out that it was her old boyfriend from Pittsfield, so they probably had gotten back together at some point near the end of the summer. I had a hard time emotionally with all of this, but that's on me, not her. Young relationships start, blossom, and then often crash. I wasn't always the best at finding ways to calm my emotions or let go of my attachments.

When my sophomore year ended, I headed back to Cambridge and got a job as a house painter for College Pro Painters. This actually turned out to be an important experience for me because I learned so much about house painting and repair, something that would serve me well for the rest of my life. College Pro hired college students and had a huge training manual on all the aspects of painting houses, outside and in. They really focused on taking good care of your tools, the importance of proper prep work before doing any painting, and making sure that the job site was always swept up and perfectly clean before leaving for the day. I was also working with a couple of old high school buddies (Suzie, who was my foreperson, and Bobby, of comics and pinball fame).

. . .

These are the things I *did*, but how was I *doing*? How was I *feeling*? Those are harder questions to answer, but fortunately for me, I had started to keep a journal a couple of years earlier for the first time in my life. Even though it felt pretty awkward, I felt the need to write (in my terrible handwriting) what I was experiencing, feeling, and thinking. It wasn't a big part of my life (I filled just one journal book over six years), but in re-reading what I wrote over that time, I can look back at my younger self and try to understand "who I was" back then (roughly ages 18 to 24).

What I can see now from that writing is that I was making friends, I was getting jobs, I was playing music, I was taking classes and learning, I was dating off and on. But also that I was often filled with different levels of insecurity and angst. I struggled with procrastination and self-control. I experienced confusion about what I was doing with my life—what direction was I heading? I was often full of indecision and doubt when trying to deal with whatever physical, emotional, relational, or educational issues I had in my life. At times, I wished I were a different person than the person staring at me in the mirror, something I know a lot of people go through when they are young.

I was a good friend. I liked people and engaged with lots of kinds of people. I was a good listener. But I'm not sure how thoughtful I was or how responsible I was when someone needed me. I wasn't good at understanding my inner self and confronting the things I wanted to change about myself. It's a challenge to confront these memories of my former self because they seem to contradict the way that I view myself now: as an outgoing, responsible, and consistently caring person, one who deals with situations professionally and conscientiously, and wants to contribute to the overall good in society.

You do spend a large part of your adult life trying to find ways to overcome your personal flaws, to find strategies to make yourself a better person, but you don't always know why you are the way you are. That makes it hard to find any kind of "roadmap" to become the person you want to be, especially when you are in your teens or twenties.

Looking back, it seems to me that what leads a person to growth and change tends to come from the relationships you have with the people that you're close to, as well as the unplanned-for experiences (good and bad) that are scattered throughout your life. That growth also depends on a willingness to notice and reflect on those relationships and the meaning of those experiences.

In 1989, a year after I graduated (apparently in a reflective mood), I wrote in my journal about what was going on in my head. The words were uncomfortable to re-read just a few years later, but as I read them now, I feel more like an interested observer of my old self:

I am trying to find peace with myself, but also truth.

Truth is guidance.
Guidance builds strength.
Strength, opportunity.
Opportunity, direction.
Direction, life.
Life, identity.

I feel like I am missing many of these. How can I make decisions about love, career, morality, fairness, that will leave their mark on me and those I come into contact with without examining why I choose one path or another? Where is the source, what is the source for my decisions and actions?

The problem comes when I don't know what is right to do, what is wrong to do, what I should do, what my brain wants to do, what my soul wants to do, what my heart wants to do.

*****

IN THE SUMMER OF 1986, as tends to happen with summers back home from college, I got yet another job: this time at a liquor store called Federal Wine, which was in downtown Boston next to the historic Old State House. The owner was Megan's father's interesting friend Lenny, who lived not too far from our Cambridge neighborhood. It was a pretty small shop, but did a good amount of business, including a regular stream of locals who were clearly alcoholics and who often came in to buy a nip or two of hard liquor.

At first, my job was to load up cases of liquor or beer on a two-wheel hand truck and deliver them by walking the streets to the local office buildings downtown. I would have to go around to the delivery entrance of the building (how would that look, with me pushing the two-wheeler right through the lobby?) and then take the service elevator. I recall one particular law office that got a full case of Heineken delivered every Friday afternoon—and they tipped well. The harrowing part of the delivery was actually just getting the boxes out onto the street: there was an extremely steep and long and narrow set of stairs leading down to the basement of the store, where you would load three or four big boxes of alcohol onto the two-wheeler and then slowly walk backwards up the stairs, lifting the two-wheeler one step at a time until you arrive triumphantly at the back delivery door and out onto the street. Later, I graduated to making wine deliveries to other cities, like Brookline or Newton, driving my car and using a book of maps to find my way to what at the time seemed like far-flung locations.

This was also the summer when friends of mine who had stuck with college right after high school were now graduating—a full two years ahead of me. Some of them were returning to Cambridge or the Boston area to find work or consider their next steps. My friends Megan and Melina returned and found an apartment together in nearby Somerville. I was heading back to UMass, but this meant that whenever I wanted to take a break from Amherst, I had a lot more friends to visit back in Cambridge.

*****

WHEN I RETURNED to UMass for my junior year, I got a small apartment on Eastern Avenue in Northampton ("NoHo"), about 9 miles from Amherst. A guy named Rob and I rented it as roommates (I had met him through friends). Rob had grown up in Boston and was (at first, at least) a lot of fun to hang out with. He had a big smile and a hearty laugh, and we had similar tastes in music and ended up throwing great dance parties together at the apartment. We shared the DJing duties at the parties and they drew good crowds (I drew fliers with little stick figures dancing their way around the edges by hand for these parties and then distributed them around town).

One night, in late January of 1987, I was standing in the kitchen in our NoHo apartment and I made a decision. I was going to completely stop eating meat. How did this change happen? As a kid, I was not what you would call "a healthy eater," with my main choices for meals being Cheerios, peanut butter and jelly sandwiches without the crust, and hot dogs. I also didn't have a history of committing to major changes in my life. But I had been influenced by readings and relationships and had been heading in this direction for a while.

I had read two of France Moore Lappe's works: her 1971 book *Food First: Beyond the Myth of Scarcity* and then the 1977 book *Diet for a Small Planet.* Both books contained well-researched and passionate arguments that hunger around the world comes mostly from artificial scarcity, caused by misuse and inefficient use of farmland. They also described the ways that the animals in the meat and poultry industries were raised, inflicting pain and suffering on them. In these books, and in others I read, I also learned about antibiotics that are used to raise cattle and about the negative health effects of consuming the amount of meat that many Americans consume, especially pork and beef.

At the same time, I was hanging out with many other long-time vegetarians, like Brian back in Cambridge and a number of people in Western Massachusetts with whom I would soon help form a reggae band. I also was getting to know some Rastafarians who "ate Ital," meaning that they ate natural, unprocessed foods —and also steered clear of meat. There were also two great student-run institutions on campus that influenced me: *Earth Foods* (their mountain of brown rice under a pile of salad covered with homemade tahini Goddess dressing lifted my spirits every time I ate it for lunch) and *The People's Market*, which was right around the corner and sold all kinds of natural foods.

What happened on that January evening was that Rob (who was a big guy from a family who often cooked big meals of delicious Haitian food) was in our run-down kitchen cooking a huge amount of beef in our wok on the stove. The smell of the cooking flesh and muscle wafted towards me and that was it for me—I had made up my mind. Since that night, I have not eaten a bite of meat. I was still eating poultry sporadically until a similar thing happened.

On Thanksgiving, a few years later, after eating a big meal with my family, I headed over to my friend James' house to have a "2nd Thanksgiving" with him, his wife, his son and other members of his family (something I had done for a few years). I still remember showing up pretty late at his house, walking in the front door, and seeing the table set up with the oversized turkey carcass in the middle, stripped of all of its life, with just bone left, and that was it—I would no longer eat poultry.

I have maintained this diet and lifestyle for almost forty years now and I've learned a lot about nutrition along the way. I've also learned to cook food from many different cultures—especially cultures in poorer countries where people often can't afford meat. Their diet has naturally evolved to include food combinations that make up for that "deficit" and with that creativity comes an incredible range of spices and ingredients and flavors.

. . .

WHEN MY JUNIOR YEAR WAS OVER, I got one last summer job back in Cambridge before I would return to college for my last year. I got a job with my friend Tom, who was an old friend of Glenn and Conrad's and someone I had gotten to know well through them. He was a talented artist, but made his living as a house painter. Since I had learned a lot through College Pro painters, I was able to be a pretty good worker for Tom, learning a lot of new and important skills along the way. I did a lot of sanding and painting, light carpentry, demolition, sheetrocking work, and floor refinishing. Every single one of these skills helped me immensely later in life and saved me large sums of money, since I was able to do work myself that a contractor would have charged ten times as much to do.

The summer of 1987 came to a close and I headed back to UMass with a full schedule of the final courses I would take in college—all "planned out." But what I did not anticipate was how busy and full my life outside of academics would be.

Selecting a record to put on the turntable in my UMass dorm room

Painting a house in Cambridge with College Pro Painters

9

SENIOR LIVING

MY SENIOR YEAR WAS INTENSE, but while my courses were as challenging as any I'd had so far, that wasn't all that was keeping me busy. That year, I became heavily involved in the Western Massachusetts reggae music scene.

At the end of my junior year, I had met several people who were musicians that were into reggae and all lived in the Amherst area (many living in mountain towns like Wendell and Leverett and Shutesbury). Some of them grew up in Cambridge and while *I* hadn't known them, some of my Cambridge musician friends did. This connection led to a few occasions where the Cambridge crew made the trip out west to play music together.

We ended up having several jams and played at a few parties. Our first gig was in May of 1987 and by the time I returned to college in the fall of 1987, we were close to forming a real band. By October, the band was starting to get more gigs and was composed of musicians Adam, Edward, Dave, Eddie-I, and me (there were other musicians who sat in at different times, but that was the core group at the time). There were a few different people who sang lead, but for a time, our main lead singer was a guy named Rob (a different Rob from my old roommate), who would drive out from Boston to practice with us and for gigs.

This crew was quite different from the Cambridge musicians I had known. It was an all-White band (later incarnations weren't) and almost all the band members except for me were dedicated Deadheads. I had a great time with them, covering some roots reggae classics and developing our own original songs and performing them wherever we could in the Amherst area. We mostly played a lot of house parties and gigs at the area's five colleges. We had great conversations along the way. Some of these guys were vegetarians and very healthy eaters who also knew how to live off the land and chose to rent homes in the woods. Some practiced Yoga or consulted the I-Ching. I appreciated the thoughtful "countercultural living" that they dedicated themselves to, and learned a lot from it.

Our band was called "The Equalites," but it was the process of naming the band that was probably the first sign that my time with this crew might not be long. A few of the other band members wanted to name the band "The Roots Penetrators," but I felt like this was some kind of joke or innuendo. Since I felt that I took reggae music seriously, I fought against it. The other issue was that most of the rest of the band was on the same page with each other in terms of taking their own approach to reggae: one that mixed traditional reggae with a Grateful Dead style. A song would start out with a solid groove, but eventually there would be very long guitar solos and the music would get louder or the tempo might change. This felt right to them, but it didn't match the style of reggae I wanted to play, that being something closer to music coming out of Jamaica. So we eventually parted ways (another way of saying "I left"), but it was certainly on good terms. I understood that they enjoyed arranging the music that way and they knew that I was looking for something different.

* * * * *

WITH A NAME LIKE "MENTOS," you know he's got to be interesting.

I had met Alwynne Mentos (who always went by just "Mentos") through The Equalites when he had gotten on stage as a guest singer with the band. He was originally from the island of St. Kitts and came to the U.S. in 1970. He had been part of the Boston Caribbean music scene for a while before moving out to Western Massachusetts and starting a family. Mentos was a great steel pan player and an even better drummer, with precision timing, decisive rolls, and a great all-around sound. He had recently formed a band called New Horizons and he wanted me to play keyboards. I would end up staying in touch with Mentos for many years after my short stint with his band. He eventually moved to Cape Cod and played music there.

New Horizons was made up of some great musicians: Mentos on drums and vocals; Patrick, a masterful reggae guitarist and strong vocalist; Adis, whose voice was as smooth as it was powerful and who also played keyboards; Dave, an expert on guitar and vocals; Boo, who played his wide variety of percussion instruments subtly and with precision; Michael, who played a deep and solid bass (Dave, Boo and Michael had all played with Loose Caboose in previous years—the band that was essentially the first reggae band ever based in Massachusetts); and me on keyboards, often playing the piano skank or organ shuffle. We were a mix of White Americans, Black Americans, and musicians from the Caribbean. The band had a style pretty close to real Jamaican roots reggae, covering songs by the likes of Gregory Isaacs, Third World, Bob Marley, Peter Tosh, Beres Hammond, and Desmond Dekker, but also doing a few original songs. I felt there was something powerful that came out of a musical conversation between people from different cultures—it gave the music an interesting richness. That mix of people who came from a Caribbean musical tradition with Americans who had studied the music and respected those traditions created an interesting sense of brotherhood, along with a great sound.

Musically, I actually felt a little bit out of my league with New Horizons: these guys were pros. The accuracy they displayed on their instruments and their vocal harmonies and the creativity that went into their lead parts—this was something new for me. But we got along great and I worked hard to make sure that I had all my parts down so that we could make some great music. My first practice with them was in February of 1988 and we gigged throughout March, April, and May, which is when I graduated and headed back to Cambridge. But there was actually even more going on musically with me at the time.

*****

IN APRIL of 1988, I also started a different band, which we called Level Vibes.

This band was made up of all UMass students: brothers Chris and Mike on drums and rhythm guitar and vocals; Mark on lead and pick guitar; Justin playing my Yamaha keyboards; and me playing the bass guitar, which I had recently taught myself. We were playing gigs at the same time that I was playing with the New Horizons. Rob came out from Boston to sing lead vocals and another singer, Kim, brought her smooth sound to lead vocals for a couple of gigs (she would later sing lead for the Equalites). This band was also focused on roots reggae, but we mostly did original songs, where I would come up with a bass line first, the other musicians would add their parts, and then Rob would come up with vocals to match. We played five or six gigs in April and May and we had a great time. This band was a bit different because these guys were all younger than me and they were up for anything, as long as they could play reggae music.

In April of 1988, I hadn't written in my journal for four months, but when I did, it was this (I don't recall what those last lines were supposed to mean, so they're open to your interpretation):

4.18.88
Playing with New Horizons and Level Vibes.
Equalites party tonight.
Otherwise, I'm lost as usual. Intermission for a life on the rocks.
Feelings for a neutral interpreter. Understanding this life form.
So?

You might be wondering what the hell I was doing playing in three bands during the hardest academic semester of my college career (and if you're not, you probably should be). In my senior year, I *still* didn't have a direction that I wanted my life to go in. I was finishing up my major, but didn't ever develop a sense of how it could be useful. I worked hard in college, but never focused on what I would do with my education to make a living once I graduated. I recognize that this is a luxury that a middle-class person might have that others may not: the time to figure out what I wanted to do without laser-focusing on finding work to pay the bills and to survive (even though I did consistently find work once I finished college). In my senior year, I was putting energy into the thing that I enjoyed and that made me feel good—playing music—more than the thing that I was supposed to be studying—high-level mathematics.

So while packing my things to head back to the Boston area, I had no way of knowing that I would indeed find a fulfilling career—but I certainly couldn't even make a guess as to what field that career would be in.

New Horizons promotional photo, c.1988

10

LET THE MUSIC PLAY

GRADUATING FROM COLLEGE in the summer of 1988 was like jumping off a grassy riverbank and into fast-moving water. I was swept into a new phase of my life, with all the studying and the unreality of a college campus swirling away behind me. As my river reached a bend, I dove right in, finding a job, moving out of my parents' house, and finding a place to live. All things considered, I would say it went pretty smoothly, even if I got a little wet.

My singer friend Rob and I found an apartment on Round Hill Street in Jamaica Plain ("JP"), a neighborhood of Boston with an interesting and complex slice of Boston's socioeconomic pie. The apartment was in a neighborhood heavily populated by Trinidadians (including our landlords, whom I kept in touch with for many years after moving on from that apartment), about a block away from the Bromley-Heath housing projects.[1] There were a

1. There is a very long and detailed article about the entire history of these projects that you can easily find on the *Jamaica Plain Historical Society* website. In a *Boston Housing Authority* article, it was explained that: "...as a result of Mildred

few of us living in the apartment, including a woman named Beth and a guy named Robin (Ravindra), himself a Trinidadian native.

Rob was an intense character who worked for Food Not Bombs, which cooked and served healthy natural foods to homeless people in Boston, often setting up their kitchen on the Boston Common. Rob was another "counter-cultural" type who was a vegetarian, very spiritual, and a great percussion player in addition to being a singer. Robin was a smart, talkative, and knowledgeable guy who had been quite a radical back when he lived in Trinidad. He was also a talented artist and craftsman, a practicing Rastafarian, and singer and percussionist.

While I had never been a religious person, I gained so much from the spirituality that permeated that house, as well as from the musicians back in Amherst and the friends who were musicians that I had gotten to know in Cambridge. What resonated with me was the depth of their beliefs, the poetic nature with which they spoke or sang of how people should treat each other, and the reverence for the natural world and for the body as the temple to God, or Jah.

Living in this apartment was spiritually rewarding, but that didn't pay the rent. I was now back working with Tom, doing house-painting, some deck-building, and starting to specialize in floor refinishing. I was learning even more skills from Tom, like using circular saws, table saws, nail guns, and crowbars. We were getting work in Cambridge, Belmont, Boston, and even painted the exterior of an historic house in Lexington.[2] But I knew I should be looking for work that would somehow make use of my college degree. I looked for math-related jobs for a while, but wasn't qualified for many of the available jobs and the ones I

Hailey's advocacy, the Bromley-Heath Tenant Management Corporation was formed in 1971 and in 1973, the BHA turned over responsibility for the development to the residents with Hailey at the helm."

2. We painted the Hancock-Clarke House, which is where John Hancock and Sam Adams were sleeping when they were awakened by the racket Paul Revere was making in the middle of the night on April 19, 1775.

could be trained in were sometimes antithetical to my values—processing actuarial tables for a big insurance company, for instance.

I was also ready to join a band and so were my Cambridge friends, the ones who had introduced me to the concept of being a reggae musician in the first place. We formed a Boston- and Cambridge-based group that at first didn't have a name and just played a couple of parties (we'd also played some parties in the summer of 1987 in Newton and Brookline, but never really considered ourselves "a band" at the time). Eventually, we got more serious and formed a larger band called High Vibes (officially "The High Vibes Reggae Band"). We had Jah T.—a precision drummer— and Brian on bass, with me and Conrad on keyboards —all Cambridge kids. Then there was Ibert on guitar (who was from the island of Dominica), Toto on guitar, Bush-I on percussion (I believe he was Jamaican), Fidel on deejay vocals (Cambridge kid originally from Jamaica), and Rocky on lead vocals—one of the singers from the Ivy Street days. We were beginning to develop our own sound, with covers of roots reggae songs and many originals. We eventually added songs in the reggae "dancehall" style, which not too many local bands were doing at the time.

Our first practices were on Washington Street in Roxbury—just two blocks from where Malcolm X lived as a teenager in the 1940s—where an older guy named Robbie had a basement space we could use. We soon moved practices to the attic of the Round Hill Street apartment, but these practice sessions were more than just a time to work on music. We ate together, we "reasoned" together[3], and we put a lot of thought into the music we were trying to create. Every time our practice was on a Saturday, Rob or I would head next door and get in line to buy some Trinidadian *roti* for the band. Our landlords (Panka and his wife Marguerite)

3. "Reasoning" is the Jamaican/rasta term for getting together to talk over spiritual or serious matters with other like-minded people.

cooked and sold this popular West Indian dish right out of their kitchen next door and many West Indians came from around Boston to get the best roti in town (they eventually moved their business—JP Roti—to a restaurant space in Dorchester and 30 years later, as of this writing, they are still thriving).

Our first official gig was a pre-New Year's Eve party: on Dec. 29, 1988, we played at the Middle East Restaurant in Central Square in Cambridge, which had started having live music seven years earlier and would eventually expand to three different stages for bands to play (main room, downstairs, corner café). I did a lot of advertising for the show and handed out fliers, excited to be bringing our sound to the people and to experience a club full of people dancing to our musical ideas. Our songs weren't yet fully formed and professional, but we were developing our own sound that we could be proud of (we also played at the Middle East in February and one of those gigs was a benefit for hurricane relief after the devastation of 1988's Hurricane Gilbert hit Jamaica). Our next big gig, on February 16, 1989, was at the famed Cambridge reggae club The Western Front. We were starting to really enjoy ourselves and the band felt like it was "on its way."

The band's name soon morphed from High Vibes into I-Vibes and over time, our personnel shifted (Sir Cecil on guitar for a time, with Natty PA on lead vocals and Kramer also on guitar) until it settled into a six-man band: Phil, who was from Allston and had fallen in love with reggae at a young age, played drums; Brian was on bass and lead vocals; Conrad played keyboards, with a focus on the lead lines; I was on keyboards and keyboard bass; the guitarist Jesse B. was a Cambridge kid with a keen sense of all reggae guitar styles—he also sang background vocals; Jem-I, who had been born in Jamaica and went to high school in Boston, was on lead and background vocals; and Fidel, who was on deejay vocals and percussion. This was more or less the core of the band from 1989 to 1994 and was a combination that found success, playing many clubs, colleges, and festivals and even doing some studio recordings.

*****

I STILL HADN'T FOUND the kind of work that would use my degree in a way that felt satisfying, but the floor sanding and house painting were soon replaced by something quite different.

One day, my friend Joni (one of the girls who danced into my room six years earlier and who was also now living in JP) suggested to me, "Why don't you try substitute teaching in the Boston public schools?" She had seen something in my personality that made her think that teaching would be a good match for me—and that subbing would be a good way to test that theory out. While I don't think I saw myself the same way that she did, it seemed like a good paying gig and so I went ahead and put in my application at the Boston public Schools central office on Court Street in downtown Boston. By October of 1988, I was getting daily calls to be a substitute teacher—for $74 a day.

Around this same time, I found a new small apartment on Lee Street on the other side of JP, near Jamaica Plain High School. My roommates were a couple named Deirdre and Al, an occupational therapist and an urban street worker, both great people. Entries in my journal were getting pretty terse at this point, but here is one from February:

Feb 20, 1989
Gigged Weds.
Practiced Saturday, in the studio Sunday.
Jam tonight, practice Tues, practice Weds.
Gig Thurs, NY Weekend.
Working as a sub.

In the years I lived there, my car—a used, but well-loved, 5-speed manual transmission Toyota—would be stolen twice, taken right in front of my apartment. The apartment itself would be broken into once, the thief coming in through the front window. The perpetrator must have been some kind of an addict because when they saw Al's big bag of papier-mâché on the living room floor, filled with white powder, they busted it wide open. I guess after taking a taste, they realized it wasn't a fortune in cocaine sitting on the floor by the potted plant. Absconding with the stereo system ended up being the consolation prize. But we loved the place for its convenient location, cheap rent, and cozy feel.

SUBSTITUTE TEACHING? That probably sounds like a bit of a nightmare if you think back to your days in high school and how you or your classmates treated subs at the time. Let me try to explain the allure, because I really dove headfirst into this job.

I'd be the first to admit that being a substitute teacher wasn't even close to a real career. But it was in a professional setting and involved presumably professionally-trained teachers and other staff in the schools who could have a real and lasting impact on the lives of the kids that attended those schools—for better or for worse. This was a very different experience from any other job I'd had up to that point.

My first subbing jobs were at high schools that were spread out all around the city. I would get a call in the morning around 6 a.m. and then have to figure out how to get to that school if I hadn't been there before. I spent a lot of time at Jamaica Plain High, Dorchester High, Latin Academy, Hyde Park High, English High, Madison Park, West Roxbury High, Brighton High, Boston Latin, the Burke, and the O'Bryant. Some of these places were in bad shape, especially Dorchester High and Hyde Park High, with broken windows, heating systems that didn't work, or generally deteriorating buildings (Dorchester High was the same building that my grandfather Manny had graduated from in 1928).

That winter I started to master what the job entailed and I started to understand the student and faculty population and the differences between the various schools. I discovered that many of the schools had significant issues in terms of how they were run, and that many of the students had more challenging lives than I had previously understood. This was at the height of the crack epidemic, which occurred mostly in inner cities around the country in the late 1980s and early 1990s. The period that I was working at Boston public schools was the most violent in the city's history. What this meant for the students I was interacting with is that they were seeing violence and drug addiction on a daily basis—and for many of them, it was present in their homes. In my time working in Boston, I went to more than one funeral of a teenager.

ONE OF THOSE EARLY MORNINGS, when I got the call to go in to sub, it wasn't at one of the city's high schools, but instead I was told to report to the Woodrow Wilson Middle School (grades 6-8) in the Codman Square area of Dorchester. The school was in an old brick building off of busy Washington Street whose student population was made up largely of Black American students, along with a significant Haitian immigrant (English as a Second Language) population, a small Hispanic population and a handful of White students (ironically, the school was named after the first U.S. president after Reconstruction to resegregate the federal workforce). I showed up that day and I did my job, as requested, following whatever lesson plans may have been left for me and trying to get the students on board with me.

The next day, an administrator called and told me that they were impressed that I was really following the plans and interacting with the students and that they would call me back regularly. Soon after, a seventh-grade math teacher broke her leg and would be out for the rest of the year. Knowing my background in math, they wanted me to take over the class for the remaining three months. After five months of subbing at different high schools around the city, I had felt like a nomad and also like an adult that was just passing through the kids' lives for a day at a time. With this "long-term substitute" job I would have my own classroom and be with the same students every day, with an opportunity to get to know each of them and for them to get to know me.

It was during this time that I got to know four or five Wilson Middle School students really well and learned that they were an aspiring rap group (the term "hip-hop" was just starting to be widely used, but "rap" was more common at the time). They rapped the lyrics to me for their song "Speakin' Out," which was basically about the violence that was happening on the streets in their neighborhoods. I was excited by what they were doing and I wanted to somehow help. I started to bring into the school my TASCAM 4-Track mini-studio recording equipment and my new Alesis HR-16B drum machine so that we could work on their songs after school in the auditorium. They called themselves "TST," which stood for "Three Stripe Tribe," referring to the three stripes found on Adidas sneakers. I also worked with a couple of their friends, including a kid named Ronald who lived in a foster home (one of a series for him) and had a rap called "The Homeless." They were only middle school students, but they were very good at what they were doing. I wasn't a professional producer either, so I guess we matched up pretty well. Their first "gig" was to perform their songs at a talent show in the school's auditorium, with the backing tracks I had made—but it would be the first of many.

By the end of the school year, the Wilson administrators told me that they were impressed that I had "survived" the year (their word, not mine) and decided that they wanted me to be a "building substitute" the following year. Being a building substitute meant that I'd be able to come into the building every day and either fill in for an absent teacher (it was a big enough school that this would probably happen every day), take on any other long-term positions that open up, or they would find other work for me to do. It also meant that I was now a staff member and so the students and I would get to know each other in a more meaningful way over the course of the year. I was also going to be paired with another teacher to do a shared homeroom duty every day, getting to know those students better than the rest.

I don't want to sugarcoat it: subbing at this school could be challenging and stressful, for a variety of reasons. But I loved it just the same and was happy to be "moving up" a bit in the world of education. I worried a little about going back to the Wilson in the fall as a day-to-day sub, given how much I enjoyed the challenge of a real class and lesson planning. But I didn't have the credentials yet to become a full-time teacher and the daily subbing would give me more flexibility around the late nights with the band (sometimes gigs would get over at 1 a.m. and I wouldn't get home until 2 a.m.).

THAT SUMMER, I-Vibes continued to get gigs, but it was vacation time for the Boston public schools, so I went back to working for Tom for a couple of months. As of August, signs of my commitment to a teaching career were showing up in my journal:

> *Aug. 17, 1989, 10:40pm*
>
> *I am 25 years old.*
>
> *I would like to: slow down, learn, contemplate, think, live, get a master's in education, teach, take musical lessons, practice, practice, practice, practice, record.*
>
> *When I'm working, even if I'm unhappy in my work, I'm happy. I live in a day. The morning comes too sudden, I need to eat. No, I need to wake up, I need to exercise my body and mind first. Start the day right, it is special, it is important.*

It was clear that I was starting to feel I had found something that felt like it had real meaning for me, that I could actually dedicate my life to. I also knew that I would have to put in the time in order to do it right.

That fall I started my new building substitute job and while I wasn't writing in my journal much anymore, I did take some notes at work when I had some downtime, which reveals what work was like:

9/22/89:

I just returned from a drive over to the Holmes School in Uphams Corner with a former teacher there to pick up books badly needed at the Wilson. The Holmes had been closed down under the deficit reduction plan. The teacher described to me the atmosphere of the neighborhood after I inquired about the two burnt out houses directly across the street from the school. She said the two houses next door had been occupied by drug dealers. Cops would make raids during the school day. One man was shot and killed in one of the houses. One day while leaving a little late from the school, this teacher was jumped, beaten and had her purse taken. This is the nightmare and sorrow that comes from drug addiction, which affects the young kids that showed up every day at this school turned ghost building.

I have become 'All-Purpose Man', cover a class here, pick up books there, call parents, Xerox manuals.

In making calls about attendance, I run into various other tasks. Several parents said their son or daughter is not in school because of a bus problem. So I discuss bus problem w/parent, get Chris H. to check on computer, talk to Joe M. about bus assignment, call parent back.

Other reasons for attendance issues: son/daughter transferring to other school, stuck in red tape, meanwhile student not attending school anywhere. Seems to be quite a lot of difficulty in transferring students.

I just spent ½ hour calling [Catholic Schools] *St. Joseph's, St. Kevin's, St. Ann's, etc. checking if students had transferred there.*

Now filling out Supervisor's Info cards.

*****

SEVENTH-GRADER AND DORCHESTER KID Eric "Rev" Johnson was a charming and good-looking kid. I'd gotten to know him pretty well in my time at the Wilson, but the specific reason I can remember what he looked like is that I saved an article from a 1989 issue of the Boston Globe that included a picture of him. The photo showed him on the witness stand in a Roxbury courtroom.

I'll let my 25-year-old self tell the story of the beginning of my connection to "Rev." This is what I wrote during a break, just after teaching one of my 7th-grade math classes:

11.15.89

Eric Johnson had showed me a wad of cash earlier.
So while the students were working on their assignment, I called him to the front of the room for a candid conversation about how he got the money. He trusts me, so he answered honestly. His answer was simply: "From selling crack" (actually, he called it some other street name). I then asked and he answered a series of questions:

How does it come?
"In sixteenths" and he went on about a bunch of numbers related to this topic.

What does it come in?
"Little baggies or wrapped in foil."

How much?
"$20 a sixteenth."

How much do you make?
"I turn $80 into $200."

Where do you sell it?
"The streetcorner on Intervale in Roxbury" [4]

Do people come up to you like shaking, and wanting it?
"Yeah..."

He volunteered:
"You gotta take it slow or you get busted. You gotta have patience, take your time."

You don't do it, do you?
"No man, you crazy, I just get it to people who want it."

You wouldn't be in school right now if you were doing it?
"That's right. Most of us don't do it."
...
The class ended and I went out to the hall to supervise and saw Jovan and asked him about his rap/dance show coming up at The Strand. Eric was coming by and I turned to Jovan and said "Jovan, don't hang out with this kid, you'll end up dead."

---

4. Intervale Street was well-known as a dangerous place where the Intervale gang resided. I ended up there late at night one time, giving one of the TST kids a ride home. There was a car blocking our way and so I was just sitting there and felt the fear that kind of reputation for violence will instill in people.

Looking back, that was probably not the right thing to say. I think I wanted Eric to know that while he trusted me and I wasn't judging him while he told me the reality of his world, it was not normal and not okay and I didn't want other kids to end up doing what he did. Later that year, two of his brothers were killed by gunfire.

The reason Eric was in the newspaper (I was shocked to see his face when I opened up the paper and saw him on the witness stand) is that he was part of a high-profile trial for the killing of twelve-year-old Tiffany Moore. The case had shocked the city when Tiffany was killed by a stray bullet while sitting on a mailbox in Roxbury. Shawn Drumgold spent fourteen years in jail for the murder, but the police had rushed to judgment and he was later exonerated, leaving Tiffany's killer free (Drumgold was awarded $5 million from the City of Boston for wrongful conviction). Eric Johnson was one of the witnesses who falsely identified Drumgold at the scene.[5]

*****

MY WORK WITH THREE STRIPE TRIBE had started to ramp up when I returned to the Wilson in the fall. In the past couple of years, my old friend James had built a recording studio on the first floor of his house in Watertown, complete with studio monitors, drums and keyboards, a window between the control room and recording booth, etc. I had already been doing some recording there with Rob and Robin as singers, so I thought we could branch out from reggae and record a little hip-hop.

I built a drum beat on my drum machine, got the bass player

---

5. At the time, I had no idea of Eric's actual role in the trial, but in researching this book I found the 2010 Drumgold court case against the Commonwealth of Massachusetts, which showed that Eric had testified that he saw Drumgold at the scene, but it turns out Drumgold was never even in the neighborhood: https://law.justia.com/cases/massachusetts/supreme-court/volumes/458/458-mass367.html

Brian to record a funky bass line (a version of a line from a Chaka Khan song), connected with a DJ who knew how to scratch and sample, and then brought all three members of TST all the way out to Watertown to record their vocals. We had a demo tape! I also took the kids to do interviews on radio stations WRBB-FM and WILD-AM. They connected with two girls from the Wilson School who became dancers at the talent shows we went to in and around Boston. I took a promo photo for them outside the school. Things were going well. Until...

Jan. 18, 1990 4:15pm

Unnatural.
It is unnatural that it is January and it is 66 degrees out.
Unnatural.
Kareem was stabbed outside the school around 2pm today by Louis R.

I was on my way out at the end of the day while Kareem was on his way in, but something was wrong. He was holding his side, bleeding, telling me it was Louis and swearing he was going to kill the kid. I helped him inside and Mr. Chestnut brought him to the nurse. I stuck around to make sure he was okay or if there was anything I could do or I'm not sure why. The ambulance came. They wheeled him outside through the front door of the school. TV cameras were rushed to the scene. "Here come the vultures" Mr. Collins says. Mr. Nathan covered the camera lens much to the protest of the cameraman.

Kareem apparently had been trying to protect a girl who Louis was harassing, and received two stab wounds to the abdomen and one to the shoulder.

My first reaction was to stay with him. Then I thought I should have gone out right away to find Louis. Revenge? I don't know.

The thought of revenge is primal but the reality is dangerous and immature. But driving home along Washington St., I scanned the sidewalks for signs of him.

This incident wasn't related to drugs or gangs, but it was made possible by the proliferation of weapons and by the cheapening of life, both of which were exacerbated by what was going on in the street. I visited Kareem in Boston City Hospital later that week. It was hard to see him in a hospital bed with IVs connected to him, but he was in good spirits and was going to recover just fine.

*****

I WANT TO MAKE SURE I am clear about my experience at the Woodrow Wilson Middle School, because the issues were not all centered on the students and their difficult lives. There were serious problems with the way the school was run by the adults in the building.

There were five administrators in the building: the principal and four assistant principals in charge of aspects of the school like curriculum, discipline, etc. Every one of the five was a white-haired Irish-American. That itself, of course, is not a problem: all the job requires is a passion for working with kids—and I certainly had no problem with older people or with Irish-Americans, many of whom have been a significant part of my life for decades. But what I came to learn was that most of these administrators had started their careers in Dorchester schools when the student population was predominantly White and I think they had difficulty adjusting over the years as the population changed dramatically. One day, I had an interaction with one of these administrators which will illustrate this all too clearly.

There was a Haitian female teacher—she was pregnant at the time—who taught mostly ESL classes to Haitian students. I generally found the Haitian kids in the school to be endearing and enthusiastic—their families had often come from the countryside in Haiti and they were excited to be in America. On this day, the ESL teacher went into labor and had to suddenly leave the building. She was having her baby—how exciting! I overheard one of those five administrators in the teacher's room mentioning the fact that the teacher had to leave. Since I was free, I said to him: "I can cover that class, if you want." His response directed at me was a shock and, honestly, disgusting. He said this: "Those kids can rot in hell, for all I care." Those words echoed in my mind for years, but on that day, I just walked away, not knowing what to say to him, and went directly down the hall to cover the class for the rest of the day. In addition to my own firsthand experiences at the school, as the students got to know me, they also opened up with their complaints about administrators and the school more generally.

I overheard a classroom aide and food-service worker having a conversation within earshot of me and spewing racist remarks (probably thinking: "a White guy wouldn't care"), including "You know *they're* gonna take over some day" (this was after they criticized a Black teacher for discussing the anthem *We Shall Overcome* with their students).

Also, at that time I was reading the book *Common Ground*, by J. Anthony Lukas, which is a highly detailed and beautifully written account of what led to the busing crisis that started in the 1970s and the ugly nature of what happened next (I highly recommend reading the book if you want to learn more). I would read a bit more of it each day in the teacher's room, but I felt like I had to almost hide the cover of the book from people. Lukas gave an honest analysis of the racism that festered in Boston and I sensed that some of the adults in my building were angry people who had been "left behind" by demographic changes in Boston and who could "lash out" at the implication that they were the problem.

I was doing everything I could to be someone that the kids could trust and confide in. I cared about them and I cared about trying to help educate them. But I have to admit that in looking back, I could be fairly criticized for not standing up and speaking out when the people around me were showing ignorance and prejudice and acting unprofessionally. It's that battle between wanting to "protect your job" and at the same time wanting to counter injustice. The problem I had was that I was at the very bottom of the chain of command—and I knew it. I could well have told the assistant principal that his "rot in hell" comment was appalling and that he should be ashamed of himself. Maybe I am the one that should have been ashamed of myself for not speaking up in that moment.

More than one teacher told me to "get out while you can," meaning that I should leave teaching in an urban setting while I'm young and find a job somewhere in the suburbs. At the time, I felt insulted by this, like they thought I would become burnt out like they were. The only student population that I knew was these Boston public School kids and they were inspiring me to become a professional teacher. I wanted to live in Boston, to get my master's in education in Boston, and to find work in Boston schools.

I-Vibes having a good time before a gig outdoors at UMass/Boston

TST promo photo: Kareem, Henry, Kevin, outside the Wilson School

11

BANDING TOGETHER

BY THE SPRING OF 1990, the I-Vibes were starting to gel as a band, writing more original music, getting more gigs, and fine-tuning everything during regular practice sessions. In April of that year, we had a show at an Irish pub called The Claddagh, which was on Columbus Avenue between the Back Bay and the South End of Boston. It was billed as a "Marathon Weekend Reggae Jam Session." We played there Friday night, another local band called New Roots played Saturday, and then Monday was a reggae deejay and dance competition.[1] As usual, I-Vibes had several special guests come on stage to deejay or sing, including two well-known vocalists, Skiffy and Mexican. That night, I met a woman named Cheryl, who'd been a big fan of reggae for several years. We talked for a while between sets and I loved her vibe. At the end of the night, I got her phone number and within a couple of days, we'd gone out to a movie

1. More info for readers that were part of the scene: New Roots was Audley Taylor and Bigga Reid's band. Monday was a dance competition with Raggamuffin International and Tappa brought his Megatron sound system for the whole weekend. There was a $2 entry fee and $500 in prizes for the dance competition. Door and spot prizes were from Talking Drum, King's Culture, and Roots International.

together, I'd hung out with her and her friends, and we had started dating.

Cheryl was from an Irish and Polish family that lived on L Street in South Boston, which was not exactly (at the time) where you would expect to find a big reggae fan. She'd grown up in Southie and gone to Boston public schools and her mother worked in the schools as a secretary. She was brash and beautiful and this was the beginning of a (sometimes tumultuous) two-year-long relationship. Cheryl had a dynamic personality and was the type of person who was quick to get to know the people around her and have influence with them. She went to most of our gigs (including traveling out of state) and even helped manage the band a little. I spent a lot of my free time with Cheryl and sometimes with her friend Dina. Dina was an artist and budding filmmaker who was from New Jersey but had gone to college in Boston and stayed after graduation. She was smart, a lot of fun to be around, and was the type of person you could talk to for hours about a variety of topics.

Also that spring, I applied to the Boston University Graduate School of Education, was accepted, and would begin to take classes there at night, part-time. I was sure at that point that I wanted to continue to work with teenagers, but I needed to do it in a way that could have a real impact on their lives and I wanted to do it in an urban environment, the only setting I had known so far professionally. Getting a master's—and the state teacher certification that went with it—was the only way to achieve my goal of teaching in the Boston public schools as a full-time teacher (eventually, I would switch to UMass/Boston School of Education, being underwhelmed with the BU School of Education).

* * * * *

SOMETIMES IT SEEMS like the English language has a word for just about everything. For instance, there is an oddly-beautiful word for when three celestial bodies form a straight line in the night sky: "syzygy" (pronounced si-zuh-jee). At one point, this was my "favorite word," if you accept the existence of such a thing. In late 1990, a syzygy of sorts happened when my previous passion for funk music, my current love for reggae music, and the connections I'd made in the music scene, all aligned with each other. This came about because Junior, who drove for Maurice, had connected with Rocky, who had teamed up with Pilot.

Rocky was a singer who I-Vibes had worked with off and on for several years. Ras Junior was well-known as the emcee for most of the big reggae acts that came into town for shows at The Channel nightclub in Boston. Junior's day job was driving a limousine, which he stored in the backyard driveway of a modest brick structure near Dudley Station in Roxbury. The building, at 27 Dudley Street, had been converted a few years earlier from a two-family home into the headquarters for Maurice Starr's recording studio.

There had been two local Boston funk groups when I was a kid that I thought achieved a depth of feeling and authenticity that was pretty close to the national funk acts from New York, Detroit, and Atlanta: one was *Prince Charles and the City Beat Band* and the other was the singer Maurice Starr. When Starr's 12-inch solo album *Flaming Starr* came out in 1980, I played it until the grooves of the record ached. It had deep funk grooves, creative ideas, and even included some slow jams. By 1982, Starr's attempts to make it as a solo artist were fading and he switched gears to co-produce and write all the songs for the band New Edition's wildly successful debut album[2]. In 1986, he created the band New Kids on the Block, specifically as a "white version of New Edition"[3], again producing and writing all the music. I

2. There were some serious issues with Starr as producer of New Edition, but the details aren't relevant to this story and can be found with a quick web search.

3. Starr thought that if New Edition had been white, they would have sold millions more of their album.

wasn't into these "boy bands," but I had been aware of them as part of Starr's increasing influence in the music scene in the late 1980s.

That fall of 1990, the singer Rocky, through limo driver Junior, had connected with Maurice Starr and booked us some time at the Dudley Street studio to record a few songs. Brian and I would be the musicians; Rocky and Jah Pilot would be the vocalists. As it turns out, there wasn't just one studio in the building, but several, each complete with mixing boards, instruments, and recording booths. Passing by the first-floor studios, we went up the stairs to the second floor, where there were studios to the left and right. After we set our instruments down, Junior took us up to the finished attic space, where Starr had his own lounge space—and we got to meet him in person.

I may have been the only one of us that was truly in awe at that moment: his solo album wasn't widely known, but I had been listening to its eight songs for the last ten years. I had a chance to tell him how powerful that album was for me, but that was about it. We headed back down to get to work. As we went into the studio on the left, I noticed four or five young Hispanic girls in the studio on the right, working out vocals for some song. I later learned that Starr was attempting to once again create a new version of New Edition: this time, a "girl band." I don't know if it ever panned out.

We recorded tracks for four songs, but only the bare bones of each (drum machine, bass guitar, simple keys, vocals). The plan was to return to the studio at a later date to add more tracks and refine the music, but somehow the studio time never got booked and the project fizzled out. So while I can't say that I have a "Maurice Starr production" in my credits, what I did take with me from that day was a recording of a straight mix of those tracks as well as a lasting memory of meeting in person someone whose music had meant so much to me as a teenager.

*****

OUR BAND PLAYED in front of a fun crowd at the Adams House dorm, twenty-eight years after my father was housed there as a Harvard student[4]. Several local reggae artists showed up that night and joined us on stage (although Harvard students weren't exactly the crowd our band and our guest artists were geared towards). The year 1991 was a busy and exciting one for the I-Vibes Reggae Band. In the spring of 1991, we had multiple gigs at the Church House Inn in Providence, Rhode Island, and also at the Middle East Restaurant, the Western Front, T.T. the Bear's, and Cantares, all in Cambridge. In August 1991, we headlined the *Rock and Reggae for the Homeless* concert at Bucksteep Manor in Western Massachusetts. In the fall, we did a mini-residency right on the water at the Outrigger Bar & Restaurant in Gloucester—sponsored by Red Stripe, the Jamaican beer company. That fall, we also played at Northeastern University in Boston and the Noble & Greenough School, south of Boston.

What kind of band were we, really? Often when a reggae band plays at colleges, schools, and other venues not used to hosting reggae, the crowd (and whoever hired the band) expects to hear covers of Bob Marley, Jimmy Cliff, or Third World, or a song like *Red, Red Wine* by UB40 (actually a cover of a 1967 Neil Diamond song). We just didn't do that.[5] We played original music. We played covers of lesser-known, but highly talented, Jamaican artists (Freddie McGregor, Sanchez, Sugar Minott, Johnny Osbourne, Luciano). And we played reggae dancehall music with guest vocalists that would come up on stage and mostly freestyle their vocals, with the band paying attention to their lyrics and adjusting the music to fit what was happening live.

In the next year or so, things would pick up even more and we would go on to play the Cambridge River Festival, the Vermont

---

4. In the early 1980s, my mother snuck into Adams House with friends to play her first ever game of squash in the dingy court in the basement. She would continue playing squash well into her 80s.

5. Actually, in 1992, we finally added a cover of Marley's Exodus for a huge show in Newport, RI, for drunken rich people, but other than that...

Reggae Festival, WERS Live Music Week, the New England Reggae Festival, Western New England College, Bryant College, UMass/Boston (twice), Nashoba Valley Ski Lodge, Mt. Holyoke College, the Pearl Street club in Northampton, the Cambridge *Youth Voter Registration Rally* on the Cambridge Common, and more clubs in the Boston area.

Our practice space improved from the Round Hill Street attic when we moved our gear to a wide open loft space that Phil the drummer lived in, right around the corner from The Channel nightclub in Boston. We later moved to a spot in a music rehearsal warehouse in the South End in Boston on Albany Street and finally to another rehearsal space in Sullivan Square in Charlestown. I looked forward to all of those practices. It was a time when I got to see people I had been friends with for years, to work on and refine harmonies and guitar and keyboard parts and bass lines. We created new arrangements for songs, introduced new songs, and arranged the set lists. It felt like we were doing something good and rewarding and creative—and doing it as a "team."

For those of you reading this who were once in a high school band or orchestra—or maybe you played in a garage band or were in a real working band—I think you know the feeling. It's that feeling you get from the ethereal tempo that's riding along underneath all of the musicians and singers who are busy weaving their parts together and interacting with each other musically. The feeling of camaraderie, of sending energy out to everyone in the audience, of seeing people dance to something you and your crew had created from nothing. Even setting up the instruments and doing sound checks felt good; calming. Perhaps the process of putting on a play would be one of the few experiences that could generate a similar set of feelings.

Looking back, I can see some parallels between the two activities that took up the most time in my life at this point. In becoming a teacher, you have to make plans for lessons, come up with new projects, be creative, interact with people, and consider your audience. You are also doing something that has a meaning and an impact on real people. In being part of a band, you have to work out the musical arrangements, come up with new music to keep things fresh, be creative, and connect with the people in the crowd. And reggae had always been a music with a message, with the potential to have an impact on the lives of the people listening to it.

In both areas, was I finally manifesting the lessons that I'd absorbed from the ways my parents lived their lives and the social activism they'd practiced and what I'd absorbed from growing up in Cambridge and my awakenings in college? For years, it had seemed like I had no direction: I was getting an education, I was interacting with people, I was working, but seemingly with no overall purpose. Maybe I had been on this particular trajectory that whole time. But I still didn't quite know where it would lead.

*****

MY WORK AT THE WILSON Middle School had been challenging, hectic, rewarding, and eye-opening. But the Wilson was a middle school and I had more interest in working in high schools. Working with high school-age kids was a double-edged sword. I liked that they were older—I could have more meaningful conversations with them. But high school kids could also be more difficult, having achieved some level of maturity and autonomy and now living in larger bodies. To me, it was worth the trade-off. In September of 1991, I started subbing at Madison Park High School, located at Roxbury Crossing, right across the street from Roxbury Community College. Another Boston high school (the John D. O'Bryant School of Math and Science) was in an adjacent building. My girlfriend Cheryl's mother worked at Madison Park and put in a good word for me and I was able to become a building substitute there.

There was one teacher I subbed for a lot ("Mr. Jones") because he was having health problems—and he was the only teacher at this school teaching higher-level mathematics. Why was he the only one? Madison Park was a vocational high school, teaching students woodworking, plumbing, food service, cosmetology, nursing, electrical, HVAC, and many other trades. But like any other vocational school, there was an important academic component to the day, and that was where I did all my subbing. There were some interesting and bright students in this school, but it had its share of problems.

Some schools would pass on their poor-performing or behavioral issue students to Madison Park. Leadership seemed to always be in flux (three principals in the two years I was there). There were drugs and weapons—despite security guards and metal detectors, weapons still made it into the building through open windows. But to me, it was all a great challenge and kept me in a school building while I pursued my master's degree, which was going to lead me to a permanent full-time position in the future.

Throughout the start of 1991, I was repeatedly called to sub for Mr. Jones' classes (he taught trigonometry and calculus and other courses). Sometimes he was absent two or three times a week. It felt frustrating to me, knowing that the students were not getting any kind of consistency in their math education. I started to get to know the kids well and they told me that he had given up teaching them, either because he was too sick or because he didn't care (it turned out, he was indeed quite sick).

At the start of the following school year, the same thing was happening—I was regularly subbing for Mr. Jones but couldn't make any decisions about the direction and approach to the courses, not being the teacher of record. The kids would be two years behind if this continued, so I decided I had to talk to an assistant principal about the situation, which I had been reluctant to do the previous year. I told her my concerns and she said that she would talk to the teacher. Two weeks later, that November, Mr. Jones retired early. I think his illness just got worse—I don't believe my speaking up had anything to do with it. The school wanted me to take over all of his classes and while I was sad for Mr. Jones (despite never getting to know him), I was happy that the students would have some stability and I would have a chance to apply my skills to making these classes work (although it still wasn't guaranteed that I could keep the job because of my lack of teacher certification).

At one point, right before getting this position, I wrote in a letter: "A substitute teacher has the craziest job with the least potential to accomplish anything." Despite that, I felt that during the years I had been working with Boston public school kids, I had made a connection with them and I could now actually make a difference; I wouldn't just be babysitting. I would plan and teach and talk and listen to my students. I would have my own classroom and some autonomy with how to run it. I quickly launched into a flurry of activities, rearranging the room, putting up interesting graphs from my Calculus textbook on the wall, working with the students on classroom rules, setting up a folder for each student so they could easily access their work at any time, and finding ways to get my students excited about what they were learning. It was possible that this job would not get fully approved, but in the meantime, I was going to do whatever I could to connect with my students—and it seemed to be working; they seemed to respond really well to me.

In the weeks following my start at that position, teachers were coming up to me, saying that their students really liked me and my class. Students were also confiding in me that they wanted to switch into my class. One day, one of my students came in and, before class started, said he wanted to write a saying on the board. I thought this was a great idea and that he should write a new one every day in the corner of the board for everyone to see. Eventually, I had three or four students writing sayings or quotes or poems on the board every day. I was feeling good about being able to apply what I saw as my creativity and caring nature and my ability to talk to people from any background and any level of math knowledge—all in a professional setting.

But it didn't last.

The headmaster, eventually, reluctantly, hired a certified teacher for the job. He apologized to me, knowing how much I had put into those classes, and, of course, I was disappointed. I think it was some combination of my lack of certification and internal politics that led to the decision. When I saw my students in the hallways afterwards, they asked me, "*What happened? Why did you leave us?*" They didn't like the change and they didn't like the new teacher. All I could tell them was that it wasn't my decision and I would have loved to stay for the whole year, but I thought it was great that they had a full-time teacher who would be present for them.

The headmaster wanted to keep me in the building, so he offered to guarantee me regular math or science work as a sub. I told him I just couldn't do that. The issue was the empowerment that I had felt in being able to make a difference in those classes—it couldn't be replaced by subbing on a daily basis in other classes where little good was happening and where I would be back to being a babysitter. Minutes after that conversation, I walked next door to the O'Bryant school and talked to an assistant principal there about working in their school. I started working there the following week.

The O'Bryant was one of the three exam-based high schools in the Boston public School system (students needed to pass an academic exam to attend). The other two were Boston Latin (in the Longwood Medical area, not far from Fenway Park) and Latin Academy (right across from Fenway Park). I loved working at the O'Bryant. It had some of the same challenges as many other city schools (one day, gunshots went off down the hall from my class), but overall, the students were wonderful and the administration was doing a good job and was supportive of me, knowing my math background and that I was almost done with my master's. At the O'Bryant I actually taught full lessons, and the students—for the most part—paid attention, asked questions, and did their homework. I was so enamored of the place that when it was time to do my student teaching, I chose the O'Bryant and ended up having a great experience there. But during the time I was teaching at Madison Park and then the O'Bryant, there was a lot more going on in my life.

IN 1991, THE BAND finally got around to recording four of our original songs in the studio (*Youth Strugglin'*, *No Tribal War*, *I-Vibes*, and *All Jah Children*). We used Post Road Productions, which was the name James had given to his recording studio in Watertown. James played saxophone on two of the songs and Brian and Fidel did the lead and deejay vocals. We had a bunch of cassettes produced at Allston Cassette, with a color cover and my contact information on the back. This "demo tape" got us many gigs, including the prestigious Vermont Reggae Festival. Brian and Fidel often tossed copies of the demo into the crowd at shows and some people still have their copy of the tape these many years later.

In late 1991, Cheryl and I had our (first) breakup. We had a lot of common interests and a lot of fun together, but I think the differences in how we saw the world started to get in the way of our relationship. I believe a lot of this had to do with the differences that arose from growing up in Cambridge versus growing up in South Boston and the corresponding cultural differences. But it's never fair for one person in a relationship to claim cause for a breakup—it's always a two-way street. In fact, we would get back together again, resuming our trips to Chinatown for delicious meals and my bike rides to her parents' home on L Street; nights she would stay over with me on Lee Street; days I would visit her at the gem shop she worked at near Faneuil Hall; and going to reggae shows and dancing all night. We were almost engaged a couple of times, but I think we both knew that, despite the good times we were having, we weren't meant to be together long-term. By late October of 1992, Cheryl and I had, sadly, broken up for the final time. But, as it turns out, I had a big surprise in store for me the following month.

An I-Vibes flyer I made, with drummie Phil's artwork

12

SHE'S BACK!

ON A NOVEMBER DAY in 1992, our local mailman walked down Lee Street in Jamaica Plain as part of his regular route. He delivered the mail to each of the small 1890s rowhouse apartments, until reaching number 21. Along with some bills and even more junk mail, he placed a red envelope into our mailbox and carried on with his route.

On my return from work, I grabbed the mail and noticed the red letter right away. I glanced quickly and saw that it was from Western Massachusetts.

Who would be sending me a letter from Western Mass?

My eyes re-focused on that upper-left corner to see who it was from.

I did a double-take.

Was I reading this right?

Yes, I was.

It was from Cori, and I couldn't believe it.

I had seen Cori once briefly, a couple of years after the breakup in 1983 that I had not wanted to happen. For many years, I had continued to take out the worn envelope with my collection of photos of her—of us—from that time. Whenever I'd look at the photos, I would remember the love we'd had for each other. It felt like that love somehow wasn't in the past, but that was just an illusion. Seeing this letter brought those lost feelings right back to the present.

It got even better: inside that red envelope was a letter on red stationery with her handwriting. In that letter, Cori reintroduced herself to me. I sat down on the couch and slowly read through it all, savoring the surprise and joy of hearing from her.

I didn't get all of this at first, but the story was that she had changed her major at Barnard College to environmental science and completed two and a half years there before transferring to the University of California at Berkeley, one town away from where she had grown up in California. She finished her degree at Berkeley and, along the way, became fascinated by wetland science. She wanted to pursue a master's in that area and ended up in Amherst to start that journey. She worked at a candle factory for a time and had other jobs to save money and then worked through her master's degree and was now pursuing her doctorate.

The girl I knew when she was nineteen was now a twenty-eight-year-old woman. She had almost gotten married. I had almost gotten engaged. We had both recently ended serious relationships. We hadn't spoken or written in nine years. But how and why did she find me?

SEVERAL WEEKS BEFORE I received that letter, unbeknownst to me, my old love Cori and her friend Tanya had driven north from Amherst to Maine to get away for the weekend. On the drive back, still enjoying the early November foliage, they decided to take a detour and pass through Cambridge. Getting out of the car, Cori found a nearby phone booth—one of the ones with the thick local phonebook attached by a wire cable. She opened the book and looked for my name, but didn't see me (or did, but wasn't sure if I would be receptive to her call). She flipped to some later pages and found Glenn's phone number (recall that Cori had gotten close to my friends Glenn, Carol, and Donny back in '83). She called him (of course, there were only "home phones" at the time) and...he picked up! Glenn was surprised to hear from her and they talked briefly before agreeing to get together that same day for lunch at Au Bon Pain, right in Harvard Square and next to "The Pit," our old hangout. The two of them spent time eating spinach croissants and catching up on each other's lives, but eventually Cori got around to asking about me: *Is Anthony still around? What is he up to?*

*****

Sitting on the couch that day, I re-read the letter that came in the red envelope, with its friendly greeting and the life updates and the expression of interest in my life. It's hard to remember all the details of that moment, but I did write back to her, and here's part of what I wrote:

> *I just got your letter and I cried.*
>
> *What I mean to say is, I got your letter, I opened it, I read it, I got to the last line, and I suddenly burst out into tears.*
>
> *It was kind of strange and kind of a release of some kind, I don't know...But anyway, Cori, it is really great to hear from you. By the end of the letter somehow I felt that we had never really lost contact with each other.*

The rest of my letter was a bit of random storytelling and rambling, but the good news is that after Cori received my response, she wrote me another letter back! In fact, it went on like this for quite a while. But we were dancing around each other. Relating how our days were going and baring our souls and writing about people we knew and what we had been doing with our lives, but trying not to imagine more. On January 11, after including some poetry by Helene Johnson in one of my letters, I wrote this:

> *...we haven't seen each other for such a long time and we're in a situation where we don't really know each other, who we've become, but for the same reason, it's exciting...and the connection still remains: that we were in love at one time. It's just been so long.*

Over the course of about two months, we would write each other about thirty letters. But a few weeks into this, we both needed to see each other in person and so we made plans for Cori to drive to Boston. She found my Lee Street address on a map and made the drive east. When she arrived at my doorstep, she rang the bell. I wasn't sure the bell was real or even if I was real, but I had to trust it and me both, and so I walked over to the door and I opened it.

SO, WHAT DO YOU WANT TO HEAR? That birds started chirping and a bright light enveloped us both in that moment? That one embrace on that doorstep confirmed what we had suspected—that we had fallen irreversibly back in love with each other? That those years of struggle and pain all melted away in an instant of pure bliss?

Yup, all that happened...

...well, there were *probably* birds in nearby trees and there *probably* was bright light from the sun...

That night, we went to Brian's place in Somerville, where

music was playing on his sound system and several friends were hanging out. As we walked into the kitchen, Mark (a CRLS grad from my class who had never met Cori) was sitting at the kitchen table with a beer in hand. He took one look at us, seeing we weren't able to keep our hands off of each other, and blurted out: "You guys are glowing!"

*****

CORI HAD TO RETURN to Western Mass, but our letters continued, just with more intensity now. We let loose our feelings and wrote poetry to each other. By February, I was writing words like the following—and feeling and meaning every word of it:

```
ENERGY & MUSCLE
I'm alive for the first time.
I connive for the  last time.
Strive      for love genuine.
Dive         in a sea benign.
Cry    at the drop-of-a-dime.
Sting       like a porcupine.
Deny that I'm trying to rhyme.

What's mine is yours / what's fine is coarse
you blink, I lose sight for a split-second...
you injure, I brace my nerves for pain...
you live,  I    b  r  e  a  t  h  e  ...
you're mad, I seethe...
```

I'm not sure how long it took, but it doesn't matter; it was inevitable at this point: within months, we were engaged to be married. I was floating through time and space, but still had to keep my feet on the ground, given the challenge of the work I was doing in the schools.

* * * * *

TEACHING in the Boston public schools and getting to know so many kids who lived in the inner city helped me to understand Boston and its people so much better—as did living and gigging in Boston.

I recall waiting one day at the Roxbury Crossing Orange Line subway stop for the train which I took every day from work. I needed just three stops to get to the Green Street station in JP and a few blocks walk from there to home on Lee Street. As I rested on a bench on the subway platform after a long day, a group of about fifteen kids came down the stairway together. They wore black hoodies over their heads, were talking loudly, and were walking close together, with the swagger that city kids can have. For someone commuting back and forth to work on the train, seeing these kids heading towards the platform might have felt intimidating. Were they in a gang? Is that why they were all together, looking menacing? Were they up to something? Were they going to start trouble? But as they got close to me, I realized that I recognized many of them. The ones that I knew were Haitian-Americans, whose families had not been here long.

What I realized was that, yes, they were trying to *look* as menacing as possible as they came down that stairway. But it wasn't because they had disdain for the working public waiting for the train or because they planned to do violence to anyone. These were kids who were trying to look tough because if they didn't, they knew that trouble would come and find them. That was the difference between this group of kids and any number of Boston gangs that were organized around criminal enterprises. But the genesis of each was probably similar. That moment of recognition was an important lesson learned, and one that stayed with me.

On January 15, 1993, trouble did, in fact, take the Orange Line train. I was on my way home as usual, having gotten on the train at Roxbury Crossing. The next stop was Stony Brook, but something would happen before we could get there. I described it all to Cori in a letter later that day:

> *I was on the train talking to a student I had had in a class earlier about turntables and different types of mixing equipment (he is a DJ). While we were talking, I noticed some kids moving around the train car together, like they were looking for trouble. All of a sudden, a fight broke out on the train. About 4 kids who looked about 17 or 18 started beating on another kid who had been sitting with what seemed like his girlfriend. The group of them sort of spun around, moving up the car as another kid tried to get them off of the intended victim. I didn't really move away from them at first because the first teacherly instinct is to break up a fight—but I made no attempt to do that, either.*
>
> *Then, one of the kids pulled out a 6-inch blade and made a move towards the kid being beat on. That's when I moved with everyone else to the back of the car. It seemed like people were flying everywhere. I looked and saw a toddler who was the only one left on the seats near the fight. At that point, the knife was plunged into the body of the kid and as the train pulled up to the stop and opened its doors, one of the kids involved started to run out the door. Then one of the kids drew a fucking gun and shot the kid trying to flee.*
>
> *At that point, people were freaking out and the toddler was still sitting there with the gunman right in front of him. I grabbed the kid and said: "Whose kid is this?!?" Whose kid is this!?!" His young father had just bolted and left him there to find his own safety!* [1]

---

1. In looking at newspaper archives recently, I found that the toddler was likely

The four guys then ran out the door, leaving the stabbed kid lying on the floor. Being several cars away, the conductor didn't know anything had happened and so he closed the doors and pulled out to head to the next station. We went to the kid and I asked him "Are you stabbed or shot?" He was stabbed in his abdomen, and was bleeding bad. A kid who knew him came over and put a cloth on his side and held it. Some idiot was yelling "He's goin'! He's goin!," like he was going to die. I told the kid, "You're gonna be alright, the ambulance is on its way, " which it wasn't because we were just pulling into the Green Street station.

I tried to comfort him while we waited for police/ambulance and got blood on my hands and my coat. It took forever for the ambulance and cops to come. The kid was bleeding like crazy. After he was taken away, I was talking with a kid I knew from the high school, who was standing on the platform, and he said that one gang was supposed to meet the other to fight at Stony Brook (the stop before Green), but they saw the kid on the train and must have just decided to do it then and there.

It was just so crazy, Cori. I mean, I know these gangs have their stupid fucking battles, but to take out a gun in a crowded subway car with mothers, students, toddlers, and just fire, it's so beyond my comprehension. Right on the subway car! It just blew me away.

In all, three kids were stabbed: two 16-year-olds and one 15-year-old, who were Roxbury and Dorchester residents. All three were members of a Mission Hill gang (in Roxbury) and they all recovered from their wounds. But 16-year-old Alex Reyes, who originally got jumped and was shot, died later in the hospital. The

---

the son of one of those involved in the fight, even though they were all 15 or 16 years old.

newspaper told a complex story of a previous stabbing of Reyes, who lived in Jamaica Plain, and the simmering feud between two gangs that led to a call for revenge, resulting in this incident on the subway. Reyes had pulled out a knife to defend himself, stabbing the kid that I later tried to help. One of the other kids then pulled the gun to shoot Reyes as he was trying to escape through the just-opened subway car door.

And the next day, life went on for the rest of us.

But the MBTA police increased security on all Orange Line trains for a while and the Guardian Angels added their own patrols. It is likely, given the nature of these things, that the cycle of revenge for the killing of Reyes carried on beyond this day, affecting more young lives and struggling families. Two weeks before that incident, I had written to Cori:

> *I think teaching and working with kids in crazy situations and running the band and dealing with musicians and club owners has enabled me to deal with people from different cultures, ages, and sexes and to be able to converse and therefore enjoy myself and learn something from each person I come into contact with.*

13

ALTERNATIVES

THE BAND HAD BEEN GIGGING together since 1989, but our lives were getting more complicated. While 1992 was busy for the I-Vibes, it would be the last year that was packed with gigs, despite scattered shows in the few years that followed. Brian got us a gig at a Fourth of July celebration bash at a fancy Newport, RI, hotel. Several hundred people were in the crowd to hear our band and we got James to play saxophone to enhance the sound. We played the same gig the following year, but other than that, things were quiet—people were working, some had kids. But we weren't done yet.

I-Vibes played Newport again in 1994 for another July 4th show and this time we had a horn section with James on sax and a guy named Tyler on trumpet. We also had four singers on stage who played percussion as well: Jem-I, Brian, Fidel, and Prince Heron (a singer that Brian knew who had some hit singles in Jamaica in the 1970s, but had lived in Boston for several years). We were still having a lot of fun on stage and off. We played four or five more shows in 1994, way down from the previous years, but the band was sounding sharp. One of the gigs that summer was the *Reggae On the Sea* event, organized by longtime WZBC reggae DJs *Robin and Lisa*. This took place, of course, on a boat that cruised the Boston Harbor. We also played *Club Europa* in downtown Boston a couple of times.

One of the Europa gigs has an interesting story behind it, so allow me to go back in time for a moment.

In 1989, the early I-Vibes band played a Fourth of July gig on the rooftop of a brownstone apartment on Charles Street in the Beacon Hill neighborhood of Boston. The rooftop overlooked the Charles River, where the fireworks were to go off around 10pm. The roof was packed, things were going well, and we were having a great time, but then things came to a screeching halt.

A young guy had climbed up on a transom window to get a better view of the band over the bouncing heads of the crowd. Notice that I said he climbed "*on* a window." The window, as windows tend to do, cracked under the weight of the curious fan and he fell three or four stories straight down the narrow vent shaft—he was trapped standing up! Once we learned what had happened, the band stopped playing and someone called 911. I recall looking down from the rooftop to Charles Street below and seeing throngs of people filling the streets. The fireworks display had ended and people had started to make their way to the subway or to parties in the area. Off to the right, down at the end of Charles Street, were the emergency vehicles, lights flashing, trying to get past the thick crowd to get to the location of the accident. They eventually made it through and ended up having to use a power saw to cut the wall out around the guy to get him safely out, although he had broken several bones.

Now back to Club Europa, five years later: we got there early to set up the instruments, climbing the double set of stairs with all of our gear. I plugged in and tested my keyboards and amps, and the guitar and bass players did the same. Phil got his drums set up and checked. Then it was time to check the vocal microphones, make sure the monitors are at the right level, get the EQ right, etc. Brian went over to talk to the sound guy that had been doing all this work with us (his name turned out to be Scott) and he seemed familiar, but it was unclear why. After Brian talked with him for a bit, the story revealed itself: "Scott" was the guy at our show five years earlier who had fallen down that shaft! He was obviously fully recovered at that point and did a great job of mixing that night—we even have grainy video from the gig—but we were all happy to learn that "4th of July transom guy" had recovered and was now a sound engineer.

THAT FALL OF 1994, Brian got us a couple of weekend gigs at a restaurant in Derryfield, NH, and for those gigs we had old friend Horace on drums and background vocals (he had been in that Ivy Street basement in 1983 and was a founding member of the I-Tones). That gig would be our last as The I-Vibes, but we got a nice recording out of it, direct from the soundboard. The band had pretty much run its course, but in the year 2000, Brian, Jem-I and I joined the band Dub Station for a few "*Dub Station with I-Vibes*" gigs at Bill's Bar on Lansdowne Street (across from Fenway Park) and at Rhythm and Spice (a Jamaican restaurant in Cambridge) and several of us would get together years later to do some studio recordings.

We had clearly found success together as a band, but in the back of my mind, I later thought: "maybe we weren't as good as I thought we were." I would say this, though: we knew what our strengths and weaknesses were. We weren't the best-trained musicians to play reggae in Boston, but we loved what we did, practiced hard, worked out great arrangements, pulled in good crowds, put on an exciting show, attracted a lot of attention from local singers and deejays, and we held tight to our values about the music. Those values were that we loved and paid respect to Jamaican reggae, we played for a West Indian crowd and not a college kid crowd, and we were always working on new original songs and introducing covers of some of the latest music coming out of Jamaica—keeping things "fresh."

For me, I just felt so "at home" with the music and the scene: when we were at a practice session, when I was hanging out at the Western Front with other musicians and singers, when we were setting up for a gig, doing a soundcheck, or starting up the first set for the night. It felt fulfilling to be a part of doing something that I loved and believed in so much and that had inspired me to learn to play keyboards in the first place.

IN JUNE OF 1993, I moved out of the Lee Street apartment. My roommates who had signed the original lease were relocating and the rent was being raised. I found a place in a second-floor apartment on Roseway Street in JP, three houses away from where the original, hole-in-the-wall JP Licks ice cream shop was (it has since become a local chain, with 16 locations in the Boston area). I had two roommates: one was a well-known local musician named Jerry (whose brother was becoming a famous Boston novelist); the other, Damien, lived in the attic and was, I believe, a heroin addict at the time. It wasn't ideal having an addict in the attic, but it was great getting to know Jerry and talking to him about music—he had a dynamic personality. Also, downstairs there was an open—albeit musty—basement that I was able to set up so that I-Vibes could do some jams and practices down there over the next year or so.

In October of 1993, after months of writing letters back and forth; of Cori visiting me in JP several times; of me visiting her in the Amherst area several times; and then the two of us becoming engaged, Cori packed her stuff to head to Boston—we were moving into an apartment together. Conveniently, the first-floor apartment in that same Roseway Street house was vacant and we grabbed it right up—all I had to do was move downstairs.

The following year, I was closing in on finishing my master's program at UMass/Boston and completing my semester of student teaching at the O'Bryant school in Roxbury, while also getting paid to do some work at UMass/Boston editing a new calculus textbook that was being developed. Once my student teaching was done, it was time to look for work once again. I scoured the newspaper job listings and eventually applied for and got a new job that I would start in September—it would be my first full-time, salaried job as a high school mathematics teacher—and it was in a very interesting setting.

Youth Alternatives

MY NEW JOB was at the EDCO Youth Alternative school, which was a small program located in Kenmore Square and was designed for "non-attending" high school kids who were living below the poverty line. What does that mean? These were kids who had dropped out of school and now wanted to go back and get their diplomas, rather than just a GED. Some of them were girls who had gotten pregnant and had to leave school; others had left school for fear of gang problems; others were on probation with the courts for some infraction or another. For me, this seemed like a perfect fit: I was ready to teach math, but I yearned for something that would have an impact, that would go beyond the content of what I was teaching.

Under an agreement with BPS, the program was set up to give the students a diploma from whatever high school they had been attending when they dropped out. This meant that these students were from all the different Boston neighborhoods. In a way, it was the opposite of my early subbing work, where I would travel to different high schools around the city—these were students from different high schools who would travel to this one building to finish what they had started. There was a very small and close-knit staff there, with only one teacher for each subject area. I remember most of them: Herc taught history. Sue was a counselor and a Boston gay rights activist. Cheryl was another counselor, who would a few years later start the influential *City Girl Café* in Cambridge. Jerome was the director.

I had an interesting mix of students, in more ways than one. Because there were so few students, my classes were not grouped by grade or ability. Instead, I had to first assess where every student was, both in terms of what math courses they had taken and what their actual skills were. I then had to find a way to individualize lessons for each student, while also coming up with approaches that would make each class feel like they were "in it together," despite doing different work.

I invented daily routines to start each class and connect kids with each other, and spent hours coming up with just the right materials that students could work through in a self-paced manner, while I spent most of the class bouncing from one student to the next and giving them mini-lessons or hints or encouragement. Two of my female students, who both had babies at home, were the most advanced of all the students. They were able to do some great work with trigonometry and they devoured all the work I gave them. But other students were quite weak and had difficulty with any level of math. Ronnel "Scooter" Adams was one of them.

Ronnel was 15 years old, skinny, and you could almost see him getting taller by the day. He was a struggling student in my class, but I liked him a lot and we got along great—he had a great smile and a lot of energy, although I noticed that at times he appeared to be angry or depressed, for reasons unknown. On Jan. 4, 1995, after he had left school for the day, around 3:30pm, Ronnel was standing on Warren Street in Roxbury and hanging out with friends. But then, some kind of fight broke out between two groups of kids and it appears that Ronnel's friend pulled a gun and fired some shots. Everyone began to run, including Ronnel and his friend, the two of them heading in the same direction. More shots rang out, this time directed at the fleeing kids, but it was unclear where they came from. Ronnel went down, hit by a bullet. According to witnesses, his friend paused for a second when Ronnel was hit, but then continued running. He wouldn't have been able to do anything to save Ronnel, who died within half an hour of being shot directly in his chest.

Police reported that Ronnel had also been carrying a low-caliber weapon, which was probably a .22. It's possible that

Ronnel had brought that weapon to school that day—our small program did not have metal detectors.

Ronnel was a young kid trying to keep up with a tough world. I attended his funeral at the Holy Tabernacle Church in the Four Corners section of Dorchester. The body was there to be viewed, but I couldn't bring myself to do so. There was mournful, yet beautiful, gospel music sung that day and the crowd was somber. It was the first murder of the year in Boston in 1995, which would see 95 more murders by the end of the year (but just 5 years later that number would be just a third of that, at 31, likely the result of good work by Mayor Tom Menino and Police Commissioner Paul Evans, but it's hard to know).

We mourned Ronnel at work and gave him the proper respect, but we had to move on. Near the end of the year, we found out that the federal portion of the funding for the Youth Alternative had been cut in half and it wasn't clear whether the program would last or not, so I needed to look for work elsewhere. But I've left out some important events that happened during this time, so allow me to back up a little.

* * * * *

IN JUNE OF 1994, at an old mansion within the Ridge Hill Reservation (an area of conservation land in Needham, Massachusetts), before friends and family from both the East Coast and the West Coast, Cori and I were married. My uncle Peter from Pennsylvania was the officiant and other family members did readings. My brother Ben played a guitar piece and my friend James' band played the music for the day. Cori and I included in the ceremony some of the poetry we'd written to each other in those letters. I guess you could say "things moved pretty quickly after that," because Cori gave birth to our son Daniel in January of 1995, just three weeks after the death of young Ronnel Adams. We brought him home from Beth Israel hospital to his new crib on Roseway Street, with plenty of ice cream around the corner.

Cori had recently landed a job in the environmental division of the Massachusetts Highway Department, located downtown, right across from the Boston Common. While I continued to work at the Youth Alternative for the rest of the school year, Cori took a few months off from her new job for maternity leave. But given the funding cuts, my job search was on.

The job that I found would be the last non-teaching job of my career, but it was still directly related to education. I was hired to be a co-evaluator of a large National Science Foundation grant, which dovetailed nicely with much of what my experience had been up until that point. The $5 million grant was for a program designed to train math and science teachers in Boston and Cambridge. It involved several institutions, many of which I had familiarity with: the Boston public schools, the Cambridge public schools, and the schools of education of UMass/Boston, Harvard University, MIT, and Wheelock College. It was an ambitious and complex program.

A professional program evaluator was hired from the organization SRI International, who then hired me to do most of the work, which she would supervise (my UMass/Boston professors had recommended me as being a good fit for the job). I visited (and wrote up reports on) innovative teacher education courses in all four colleges, as well as meetings of college staff, meetings of Boston and Cambridge public school staff, and meetings of the grant oversight committee. I also interviewed classroom teachers and professors and the program organizers. The job was to co-author a lengthy annual report detailing the progress of all this work, which was a multi-pronged approach to improving math and science K-12 instruction in the Boston and Cambridge Public Schools. We would point out strengths and successes and indicate areas for improvement.

I got really into this job, honing my interview and writing skills, meeting a wide array of interesting people, and learning a lot about how these programs worked and what was happening in the public schools that were part of the program. The traveling was also great, because I did a large part of it by bicycle, zipping around to the colleges for night courses and to the public schools during the day. Whenever possible, bicycling continued to be my mode of transportation—it was just so much more fun biking through the city than driving. At this point, Cori and our son Daniel and I had moved to Arlington, not far from Cambridge, so the biking distances into Boston actually grew quite a bit.

This interesting work helped increase my desire to get back into the classroom myself. So while the grant would continue (it was a five-year grant), I began to search for a teaching job that would bring me back to what I now felt was my real purpose in life.

In the summer of 1996, I put in applications for teaching jobs in urban districts like Boston, Cambridge, Somerville, and Brookline, while still keeping up my work on the NSF grant—I didn't want to burn any bridges. I got a few interviews, but for some reason, I had a hard time finding a teaching job. I also included a few suburban schools in my applications just to be as thorough as possible. As the fall arrived, I knew that the job search for that school year had come to an end.

But I was wrong.

* * * * *

FALL ALWAYS BRINGS CHANGES, especially in New England. The leaves would soon drain their green pigment, leaving orange, brown, and red. The maples have always been my favorite, with their elegant and proud shape. The hot and humid days would make way for chilly nights and mornings, great for running or biking. One day in that first week of September also brought the moment when a new member of our family would enter this world. Cori gave birth to Adam in Mt. Auburn Hospital in Cambridge, the same place that my father had started his life sixty-one years earlier. Daniel now had a brother.

Two weeks after Adam's birth, with a lot going on in our

household, I found myself thinking back to what I knew of the suburban town of Concord and realized: not much. To me, Concord was where Walden Pond existed—that was about it, and that was enough (at the time, I perhaps knew the phrase "Lexington and Concord," but not really its significance). My parents had taken me and my brother to Walden when we were little and as a young man, I had biked or motorcycled there with friends to take a dip. I had otherwise never spent any time getting to know Concord—or any other suburban town, for that matter. They didn't interest me. In a way, that turned out to be fortunate.

A veteran mathematics teacher at the well-regarded Concord-Carlisle High School had taken ill and would need to leave her position to get treatment—she was essentially retiring early. It was the third week of September, 1996, and the school needed to find a qualified replacement quickly, including someone who could teach an Honors Algebra 2 class. That application I had filled out months ago popped up and they called me in for an interview. The advantage that I had was that I had no interest in teaching in a suburban setting, but I decided to go in for the interview anyway. This took off any pressure that I might have otherwise felt to "pull out all the stops" in the interview. Where I might have tried too hard to impress the principal or other members of the interview team, instead, I was cool as a cucumber.

When they asked about my previous work as a teacher, I had fun telling them about all the innovative ideas I had come up with, and I gave specific examples of connections I had made with students. I was able to convey my enthusiasm for teaching and my approachability as a teacher. As a math major, I also had all the qualifications to teach whatever courses they might throw at me. I left the building that day feeling pretty good that I had gotten some good interview practice. But then the next morning, I got a call—it was unanimous: they wanted to hire me for the job.

I still had a decision to make, because no part of my life plan had ever involved teaching in a suburb twenty miles outside of Boston. I talked with Cori about all the pros and cons, needing help to figure this one out. My passion was for working in an urban setting, where the students were the "types of kids" I knew, felt comfortable with, and felt I understood. What would be the advantages of teaching in Concord?

On the day of the interview, before leaving the building, I had been introduced to members of the CCHS Math Department. They seemed dynamic, interesting, and interested in what I would bring to the department. CCHS seemed like a collegial place, something I hadn't seen enough of in Boston. There was an upbeat feeling. This is no surprise—who wouldn't be upbeat, with a healthy budget (resulting from the high real estate tax income of Concord and Carlisle), a supportive principal, students from stable and comfortable homes who weren't struggling to survive and so were generally more focused on their studies and their futures, teachers with a "four class load" (in most urban schools, teachers taught five or even six classes, often with 30+ students) and a great contract with excellent pay?

My mind pulled me in both directions. On one side was working in urban schools with challenging conditions, but where the work was more spiritually rewarding. On the other was a school that would be professionally challenging, but would be less stressful and allow me more room to grow. Of course, the other factor was, honestly, I had only one job offer to consider at that time.

I signed my contract with CCHS the next day. I had made my decision and would start almost immediately. The next day, I would observe the teacher in her classes for two days before taking them over myself. When I arrived at CCHS to do my observations, having left Cori, a newborn, and a toddler at home in Arlington, I walked from the parking lot and up a ramp to the doors to the "L-building," and then down the hall to the Math Department. The strongest memory that I have from that moment is having this odd feeling that I'd "never seen so many blonde people in one place!" Thinking back, I suspect that not that many of the students had blonde hair, but I was so used to working in the Boston public schools, where White students were the exception and not the rule, that the contrast overwhelmed my senses. Despite the shock to the system, I kept walking down the hall towards my new classroom.

*****

What did I do next? I spent close to the next three decades teaching at Concord-Carlisle High School, getting to know the school and the students, my colleagues and the administrators, the curriculum and the expectations, the culture and the vibe in that building—and I started to finally become the best version of the teacher I imagined I could be, just not *where* I imagined I would be.

At EDCO Youth Alternative, in Kenmore Square

PART II: BEING

14

MUSIC

WHEN I STARTED WRITING THIS BOOK, I wasn't sure what it was going to be about. I *thought* I was going to just record and put down on paper the events that happened over the course of my life. But over time, the goal of my writing began to evolve into something more cohesive than that. The writing process itself helped to reveal a new purpose: to delve into how I formed my identity and to reflect on how *anyone* forms their identity. I wanted to answer questions about what parts of identity had been there all along and what parts arose through influences, through thought and reflection, through relationships, and through experiences and events.

After my second son was born and I'd taught for a few years in Concord, much of my adult identity had found its way out of the darkness and had spoken up and asserted itself. This does not mean that I had "figured it all out." Some aspects of my identity were probably formed over time for the purpose of masking qualities in myself that I didn't like. Some are still works in progress.

I think I am a good friend—but I don't think I'm very good at societal traditions that can comfort people and make them feel appreciated, like showing up to a person's house with a gift, or sending birthday greetings and "get well" cards. I'm usually a good neighbor, but sometimes the neighbors that I still consider "new," and haven't gotten to know yet, have already lived next door for years. In my rush and excitement about some interesting project I might be working on, I'm sometimes impatient with people when I shouldn't be. I've also had my share of leaping without looking.

When you know there are parts of yourself that you'd like to change (I hesitate to call them "faults"), you have some choices. One approach is to work to change those things. Barring that, you could find ways to compensate for the qualities you wish you didn't have but have trouble shedding. Another choice, of course, is denial. But denial's happier cousin would be acceptance. Maybe you shouldn't beat yourself up about things that are difficult to change and don't negatively affect the people around you.

Regardless of any work I had left to do on myself, once I hit my thirties, many of the qualities I wanted to change about myself had indeed changed. I had gotten past many insecurities and vulnerabilities. My values and beliefs, my sense of ethics and charity towards others, the seeds of which had been planted long ago, were part of my family life and my work life. In other words, my identity had in large part solidified. The same thing was happening all around me with friends and relatives that were my age. Some became writers, bike mechanics, architects, teachers, software engineers, and social workers. Others struggled and became homeless or drug-addicted. Still others died young. Some were still looking for the path that would lead them to fulfillment and purpose.

Given that this book is about *forming* my identity, in order to tell the rest of my story, it wouldn't make much sense to continue going through "what I did next" or to "list my accomplishments," which have little to do with how my identity formed. That also sounds a bit like a resumé to me, not an interesting chapter of a book. For this reason, the remainder of this book it will contain a series of shorter reflections on what that process of forming my identity ultimately resulted in. In other words, how in my later life I expressed that found identity.

I will start by saying a few things about music.

*****

MUSIC TOOK A BACK SEAT to family and work for the next two decades.

Well, I don't mean *music* did. Music has been a significant part of my life since I first heard records playing in my parents' living room, and it is still with me every day. From the Beatles to the Kinks, from Cameo to Funkadelic, Bob Marley to Steel Pulse, Oscar Peterson to Thelonious Monk, the Mighty Diamonds to Buju Banton, Lavay Smith to Madeleine Peyroux, Mayer Hawthorne to Capleton, and Stevie Wonder to Stevie Ray Vaughan, I continue to need music in my life. It plays alongside the story of my daily life. But *playing* music in a live setting, swimming in the music that is created by my own hands and with others around me, working and sweating together with band members sharing a mutual trust in each other—all of that *playing* of music took a back seat.

Until 2016.

Recording Music

I'D KEPT IN CLOSE TOUCH with members of the band, despite being busy with a career—especially Brian and Jem-I, but also Phil the drummer. I hadn't seen much of Jesse, though (the guitarist and background vocalist for the I-Vibes). In 2016, I reconnected with Jesse at his apartment in Somerville and suggested we get together for a some musical jams. I had a drum machine to keep time for us, he had a bass and guitar, I had my keyboards, and my kids were old enough that it was much easier to get away on the weekends for these sessions. Over the next couple of years, Jesse and I started working out a bunch of covers, created a few new originals, and brought in some other musicians to play with us. It wasn't "serious," but it sure was fun.

Eventually, we started recording music and getting to know the recording software on Jesse's computer. We came up with a few new originals and recorded them, got Brian involved (he was also starting to do his own recordings), and the music started flowing—and sounding better and better. I also did some searching and was able to find where Horace was working and showed up one day at his job in Central Square to reminisce about the old days, but also to suggest that he could do some drumming with us (he was also a singer and songwriter and would eventually work with us on his original music). Music had returned to my life in a way that felt enriching. But even more importantly, it involved creativity in a way that was new.

I installed the same music software on my computer at home and began writing and playing my own music. At first, it was just simple drum beats with a keyboard bass and other keyboard tracks. Eventually, I got a used guitar, some percussion instruments, a bass guitar, and a microphone for vocals. In about 2018, I started to have a burst of creativity, the likes of which I'd never before experienced.

As I've mentioned, I wasn't a highly-trained musician, so while I did introduce a lot of the new songs in the I-Vibes days, it was mostly just a bass line and the accompanying chords. I wouldn't really have called it "songwriting." But this was different. I was working through drum parts carefully, coming up with horn lines and organ parts that would complement vocals, thinking about chord progressions—and eventually writing my own lyrics to create original and complete songs.

To be clear, I had never once been a singer in any of the bands I played in and certainly didn't consider my singing voice to be good enough to record. So at first I worked with a range of singers like Brian from I-Vibes, Jesse, Horace, Jem-I, Journalist, Skiffy (a

Jamaican singer I had met back in my I-Vibes days) and eventually the singer and Vermonter Sista Pam, who was the original manager of the Western Front reggae club and who had a powerful voice, but had never recorded as a lead vocalist.

All of this work transformed my mindset, giving me a new sense of creative exploration that I hadn't felt before. This, along with Sista Pam's encouragement, drew me toward making some solid attempts at songwriting as well as singing my own lyrics. This wasn't about me trying to be a "great singer," but more about being able to, after all these years, express myself through music and fully engage with the joy one can get out of being as creative as possible, whether musically or in other areas.

I realize as I write this that throwing myself completely into a musical project, fine-tuning it, learning the technology associated with it, and collaborating with others on it—all have echoes with my earlier life. There are traces of it all in what I was doing when I collected coins or baseball cards or comic books, even more so in how I engaged in building electronic circuits, writing code in high school, or being part of rebuilding a pinball machine. There was even a connection to the multi-day bicycling trips I later planned and the new courses I developed at Concord-Carlisle High School (more on this later).

Also, when I started writing lyrics and singing vocals, the lyrics had a focus on ideas and values that had been part of me for a long time. While a couple of the songs I've recorded have been fun dance songs, most focus on themes of peace, justice, racial harmony, personal reflection, the failure of political leaders, etc. I can't help but think that the ways my parents lived and how they raised me, which led later to my own awakenings (even if it took a while), was coming through in how I was expressing myself lyrically.

Music History

A BIG COMPLEX PROJECT centered on different cultures and on music and local history? It was too good to resist.

I had for many years been the "keeper of history" not only for my family, but also for the bands I played in. I was the one who took the pictures at shows, who brought the boombox to record, and who saved all of those historical artifacts along with the posters, t-shirts, newspaper articles, and personal memories. I had been posting some of these memories to social media for quite some time, but around 2020 a friend suggested that I create a group dedicated to the history of the reggae music scene in Boston, a scene which had its start in the mid-1970s, not long after the music itself was born in Jamaica.

So, "with a little help from my friends," I created the *Reggae Dawn* group, with a focus on the twenty-year period from 1975 to 1995 in Boston. I began posting artifacts from my own archives and then started receiving donations from some of the original singers and players and others from that time period. The project turned into a vibrant community of people from around the country (and Jamaica and the U.K. and other places), focused on sharing memories of what the unique Boston reggae scene was like, what it offered people, and how it impacted musicians, singers, club owners, arts reporters, radio DJs, and fans at the time.

People began sending me their own archival materials to be processed (the lion's share came from the I-Tones' keyboard player Abdul), such as posters, cassettes, vinyl, photos and video recordings. I used my computer skills to process hundreds of hours of music from cassettes, make simple videos for each, and post them online. I scanned and digitized posters and photos and negatives and contact sheets. I gathered stories from people and posted their narratives. Eventually, this became too much to keep track of and too ephemeral for social media, so I built a website dedicated to showcasing all that the scene meant to people and included the recordings, video, images, and everything else I had collected. Pages of the website (reggaedawn.com) are dedicated to women in Boston reggae, the history of each reggae band in this time period, Boston reggae radio, the famous Western Front reggae club in Cambridge, newspaper clippings, local record shops over the years, and a timeline of all of this.

At one point, an archivist at the Boston Public Library got in touch with me, having heard about my collection. They wanted to put on a presentation about the Boston reggae scene. Later, the Massachusetts Historical Society contacted me and I ended up helping them connect with key players from the Boston reggae scene. The MHS planned on doing a series on different Boston music scenes from different time periods (folk in the 60s, funk in the 70s, reggae in the 80s, and rock in the 90s). Since I knew the people and the scene, they wanted me to sit in on the interviews, of which we filmed several. Sadly, both projects ended before being completed, one due to administrative changes, the other because of budget cuts that removed the administrator of the whole project. But the formerly shy kid in me was surprised and thrilled to discover that I was a good interviewer and that I could be of help to others and contribute to an area that people had such an interest in.

As an adolescent, I was a collector of things. I shared that passion with friends, but the collections were "for me." I was nostalgic and enjoyed sitting back, taking in, and imagining myself in the fascinating past. As a high school student, I was capable, but not particularly motivated, unless it was something related to my limited passions: biking, pinball, and comics. I see now that the most joy, for me, has come from applying my passion to some major project (the more complex, the better) that connects with my interests, but also affects others in some uplifting way. While I didn't really have the tools when I was younger to make this kind of thing happen and probably didn't have the confidence to be the person that could bring joy to others in this way, perhaps it was just a matter of time and patience to allow my interests and my skills to find each other in a productive way.

Working out some studio music in Cambridge

15

BIKING

I RECENTLY TRIED TO CALCULATE something that was incalculable. It was going to be impossible to do accurately, but I'm okay with that.

I came up with this result:

87,950

This is my estimate of how many miles I have ridden on a bicycle over the course of my entire life. It comes in part from estimating the miles that "everyday rides" contributed: rides with friends, commuting to school, commuting to work, running errands, going shopping, going out to see shows, taking friends on tours of the city, and riding for fun.

For much of my life, I've chosen to avoid using a car whenever it was "feasible"—but I had my own definition of that term. This meant that I was using my bike in some unusual situations, like picking up a large bag of bark mulch from the hardware store, or going to a late-night reggae show in Boston in January, or biking fifty miles round trip to attend the end-of-year Math Department party. To get an estimate for these "everyday rides," I used a relatively low annual mileage amount for when I was in elementary school, followed by increasing amounts as I grew into adulthood.

In addition to my daily bicycle riding, I also invented a series of my own "bike projects" for which I had more specific mileage amounts recorded:

2002-2019—*bike touring trips that I planned and executed:*

60+65+290+250+350+260+205+ 305+470+ 380+350+600+260
= **3,845 miles**

2012—my "*every day for a year*" project: **2,430 miles**

2019-2020—my "*every street*" projects:
282+174+267+231+80+123 = **1,157 miles**

2021-present—my "*every town hall*" project: **2,200 miles**

* * * * *

I've mentioned that my great-grandfather on my father's side came to Boston from Lithuania when he was a teenager and soon after started a small bike shop called Hub Cycle in the North End, a business which carried on for another 75 years. But my great-grandfather and great-grandmother and my grandfather and my grandmother—none of them were really into biking. It was the family business, not the family sport.

My parents, however, did bike to work, my father biking five miles each way for close to fifty years. My mother biked to do all manner of things, and both of them set off on significant bike trips locally, nationally, and internationally. My older brother Ben has also been a devotee of using a bicycle for everyday travel and errands for many decades. So my interest and love of bikes certainly has a backstory; it had a catalyst. I think, however, that there is another part of my nature that makes me want to "take things further." And this is what I did, starting in 2002.

*****

MY FIRST "LONG" BIKE RIDE AS AN ADULT was in 2002 as part of a fundraiser for *Bikes Not Bombs*[1], an organization and a cause I firmly believed in. The ride started in Jamaica Plain and made a southern 60-mile loop, returning to the starting point. I learned a lot from the challenge of that ride, and so a year later, I biked by myself the hilly 65 miles to Greenfield, NH, to visit my old friend Carol and her husband Neal.

That would be the beginning of my system of planning longer and longer trips to go on every summer while I was off from school, usually solo and always with whatever gear I needed, loaded right onto the bike. Two of the longest were my solo ride in 2015 to Baltimore to visit my old friend Melina, which was 470 miles, and the ride I did with my son Adam to Toronto in 2018, which was 600 miles (I had biked to New York City and circumnavigated Massachusetts with my son Daniel in 2012 and 2013). There are many stories to tell about these annual adventures, but that wouldn't really fit with the purpose of this book, so if you want to hear more, you'll have to find me and ask about them!

THOSE SUMMER TRIPS LIT A FIRE under me that led me to some other biking projects—ones that I could do year-round. I found

1. Located in Roxbury, Bikes Not Bombs (in addition to other projects) collect old bikes and both train city kids on how to fix them (handing them the bike when they're done) and sending trucks filled with bikes to Africa, Central America, and Caribbean, allowing people without the means to have convenient transportation.

the process of coming up with an idea that's complicated, planning how to implement that idea, and then dedicating myself to completing it—all exhilarating to me. Here they are:

In 2012, I decided to bike every single day, always five miles or more, for 366 days straight (it was a leap year), rain or shine—or even snow. Sometimes I'd have to do it early in the morning, sometimes I'd have to get the ride in before midnight. Sometimes I would bike the minimum five miles, sometimes I'd be on some trip somewhere and do 70 miles that day. At one point during that year, I was in California to visit Cori's family and so I bought a cheap used bike to ride for a week. Later, I was in St. Louis for a robotics competition that Daniel was in, and so I rented a bike for two days and ended up doing a long ride along the mighty Mississippi on one of those days.

In 2019, I decided to ride on "Every Part of Every Street In Arlington" (my "REPESIA" project), which totalled 282 miles (obviously, there is no way to ride each part of each street only once, so a lot of these miles came from "getting there"). I followed that up with riding every part of every street in neighboring Belmont, then Winchester, Somerville, and finally Charlestown (I actually rode about half of Medford's streets, but I got sick of the city and so abandoned the project—although I still might do Cambridge or JP or Roxbury some day).

In 2021, I began my project of biking to every town hall and city hall in Massachusetts, always starting from my home in Arlington. There are 351 cities and towns in our state and as of this writing I have biked to 151 of them, which has taken 2,213 miles to accomplish (of course, once I'd biked to a lot of them, there were a lot of miles just to get past those towns to the ones I hadn't reached yet—it adds up!)

These projects seem to have a bit of an echo of my former self, but also a developing sense that I wanted to conquer things that a young Anthony would *not* have attempted and would have, in fact, been quite resistant to.

Some observations about bicycling in general and my projects in particular:

• When I was a kid—and even later as an adult—I would sometimes look up at birds flying in the sky and think: *What is that like? What must it feel like to soar in the sky, to float on the air, to watch the earth below and all its inhabitants while you glide through low-friction space?*

Only recently had I realized the answer. Especially on a new, smooth, country road with few cars, the bicycle rolls by itself, the rider sometimes swaying left and right to feel more alive, to take advantage of the space, watching as the countryside or city neighborhood floats by. Bicycling allows you to get a taste of what flying through the air must feel like. It's part of why I bike year-round and what drives me in my adventures. When I head out on my bike after some period of time "off the saddle," I get the sense that I'm experiencing once again what it was like to be a kid and to have the freedom to bike anywhere and to glide around the world.

• The bicycle itself—the machine—feels special for a reason that my younger self probably wouldn't have been able to articulate: it relates to design and construction.

Adults tend to want cars. Cars are powerful. Cars have beautifully designed exteriors. Their exteriors help cut down on wind resistance and protect internal parts and people from the elements. But they also hide every working component that makes the car a moving vehicle. The same is true for airplanes and TVs and computers and smartphones and yes, even the human body. For each, the inner workings are purposely hidden so that you can only consider and work with the internal parts with some effort. Not so with a bicycle.

Bicycles have, from the very start, been designed so that the components are *not* hidden from sight, afraid to be found out. Each part is out in the open and proud of it. At a glance, you can see the cables, the spokes, the derailleurs, the sprockets, the crankset, the rims, and the nuts and bolts that keep everything together. It bares itself completely to the elements and was designed to handle them. This is part of what I love about bicycles. You can watch as your gears change, as your chain turns, and as your brakes squeeze. If something goes wrong, you don't need to open the hood; you just hop off your bike and take a look. This matches with how I want to access the complexity of the world: in a direct way, with the parts staring right at me and inviting me to them so that I can study and contemplate and alter them[2]. Those parts (without any external energy) use the best that the laws of physics have to offer in order to make something magical: they allow the human body to go faster and further than its legs could ever do.

• I've realized that, while my resistance to travel when I was young (which has lasted into adulthood) was partly in reaction to being pulled away from the local thing I wanted to be part of, it was also a resistance to "being told where we're going and what we're gonna do." I know now that I need to be the one to make a plan. That I need a challenge and if that challenge is a physical one, all the better. That in my travels, I am drawn towards cities, but passing through rolling countryside to get there enhances the city experience. My bicycling projects have been a way to do the

---

2. Writing code also has satisfied that need of mine to see the internal parts of how things work.

kind of travel that fits with whatever weird combination of needs and inspirations have developed in me since I was young.

There's also a certain amount of suffering that goes with a major, multi-day bicycle trip—just like when I was a kid on the Keet Seel hike. I realize now that there can be a place in one's life for something that is challenging and can knowingly lead to suffering—it can be a feature of a journey, something that inspires by breaking a person down to some fundamental part of their humanity.

• One of the greatest joys of my life was teaching my two sons to ride a bicycle at a young age. It felt like the first time that I was teaching them something really important that could affect them for the rest of their lives. It also involved the joy of watching the excitement in their faces and their voices when the bicycle did not fall over, and they were able to just...keep...going...

Biking from Arlington to Toronto

16

TEACHING

I ENTERED THE WORLD of teaching accidentally; it had never been part of any plan. I do feel like I was fortunate in the sense that my parents didn't pressure me (much) to find a profession right out of college. I didn't have much professional ambition—I just wanted a job so I could have an apartment and do what I loved to do in my personal life. Maybe this is why I was able to find the thing I loved—I had plenty of time to stumble around in the dark until I could find the light switch. But once I realized my passion was for teaching—even as I was subbing, before I knew where this would head—I put everything into it. It felt like something that required thoughtfulness, planning, strategy, intelligence, empathy, a personal touch, and a willingness to tackle complexity and react to the unexpected. Sounds good to me! In some ways, this is wildly different from who I was when I was younger, and in other ways, it's where I was heading all along.

Some observations on about teaching:

When I began teaching at CCHS, I was a little nervous, but

mostly I thought I had the personality and all the tools I needed to be a good teacher. In other words, I thought I "knew what teaching was all about." It took a while to realize that the ability to explain complicated concepts and to do it in a clear way was fine, but those skills were not at all sufficient to creating a lasting impact on kids and being able to reach every student. So I dove into finding innovative teaching ideas and adding them to my routines.

I developed a thirst for exploring new ways to look at the content I was teaching and delving into any connections and applications I could find that would feel real to my students. I, along with most of my colleagues, embraced the idea that kids need to *engage in* ideas, not just receive them. Kids needed to explain ideas to other kids and listen when their peers do the same. They needed time to think and try to make sense of concepts before trying to apply them. Students yearned for things to make sense, sure, but they also wanted to feel like what they were studying mattered. And that they mattered. I committed myself fully to these ideals for the rest of my career and was able to work with some incredible colleagues who taught with me and grew right alongside me.

I've mentioned some "mistakes" or "stupid things" I did when I was younger. I tried as much as I could to remember this when working with students who were, for whatever reason, doing things that might upset a teacher. If a student copied a homework assignment or cheated on a quiz or a project, or said or did something inappropriate in class—these were things that did need to be addressed and there needed to be consequences. But a teacher needs to remember how *human* they were as a kid when they were in school—that their brains weren't always developed enough to always make the right decision. If they can remember this, then whatever the behavior is, it should be addressed without anger, without judgment, and without assuming that it reflects on the kid's moral character, just as you wouldn't want them to judge your younger selves for mistakes you made.

. . .

I've felt compelled since my early days of teaching to go beyond the regular, traditional curriculum, which always felt too proscribed, always a bit out of date, and usually not tailored to the students I had in front of me. I didn't fully know this at the time, but both of my parents had thought the same way when they had engaged in their teaching.

I mostly knew about my mother's work as a teacher in alternative public high schools in Cambridge and Watertown, but I hadn't realized that even within those alternative programs, she wanted to create her own courses, to tailor her instruction to the students she had in front of her and to teach in a way that matched with her values. She created courses with names like *Interviewing, Language & Power,* and *Assertiveness.* She almost never used a textbook, including in the college writing and journalism courses she later taught or in the anti-racism workshops she led. My father taught courses in his field at Harvard Medical School, but his most lasting legacy was the course he created and taught for twenty-nine years that was focused on social issues in biology. This course pushed budding science researchers to go beyond their content-focused training and to consider the complex responsibilities to society that should come with the power of doing scientific research. The course was a new idea and the curriculum was constantly being updated to keep up with new developments in science and their implications for society.

As a teacher at CCHS, I carried on this tradition. Within a couple of years of starting there, I had picked up a new course called *Advanced Topics in Mathematics* that had been taught for the first time just the year before. I spent the next fifteen years developing my own curricular materials for this course from scratch. In my mind, it was a class for seniors who were not interested in taking calculus or statistics, but eventually students from a variety of backgrounds ended up becoming interested in it and started to sign up for it.

The idea of the course was to introduce units on very real-world applications of mathematics and to expose students to the joys of mathematical topics not typically taught in high school. It started slowly, but eventually I developed brand-new units on number theory, encryption systems, networks, the mathematics behind the Global Positioning System, how chaos theory plays out in mathematics and science, the mathematics behind barcodes and "2D symbologies" (one of which is the now-ubiquitous QR Code), deep explorations of fractal geometry, as well as other topics that came and went (at some point, I had developed too much curriculum and had to pare down to be able to fit it within the school year). I spent hours scouring used bookstores in Arlington and Cambridge for books on these topics and more, building a formidable library and getting excited every time I found something I thought would be perfect for my class.

The Advanced Topics course came to an end partly because I had come back to "my first love," which was programming. I decided to introduce a course in Java programming, a language that I didn't know, but was excited to learn and pass on to my students. That course quickly became popular and I began to expand my offerings, teaching myself (and then the students) Python, HTML, CSS, JavaScript and dabbling in other languages. I also started an after-school *CCHS Coding Club* (after I had run a *CCHS Bike Club* for a couple of years).

Eventually, I had enough students sign up for my computer science classes that I was no longer teaching any mathematics courses at all and had essentially created my own Computer Science Department–with just one member. The best part of every coding course I taught was the four-week period at the end of each semester, which I left for the students to create a complex and significant "final project"—something from their own imagination and of their own design. For some students, this was a real struggle, but for me and the students, it was collaborative, creative, and fun—the best four weeks of the school year, every time.

I was thankful that my department and my school system allowed me (and plenty of others) to innovate and experiment and go deeper with everything I was teaching, and to allow me to continue to embrace complexity rather than stick to the status quo—in other words, to follow the trajectory that I seem to have started on as a young Cambridge kid.

What is the fuel that keeps teachers going for decades? What pushes them to creativity and innovation? I believe the answer can be found in one's students and colleagues.

High school students are filled with angst, but also wonder. They may seem too focused on grades, but they also want to learn something that feels important and interesting. They sometimes can't behave as expected or can't stop talking in class, but they also have energy to spare: a good teacher can help to focus that energy on learning just about any subject imaginable. In my life, I've never memorized lines from a play, a poem, or a speech. The only thing I've ever dedicated myself to memorizing is the names of my students—hopefully before they show up for the first day of school. High school kids have a lot of needs, starting with wanting to be seen and heard and known, and that begins with knowing their name and pronouncing it correctly. They also have complex lives and sometimes behave in ways that surprise or upset you. But most often, there are reasons for those behaviors that can only be discovered by getting to know the student and building as much trust as you can with each one.

Each of my fellow teachers at CCHS were dedicated, thoughtful, and caring educators, and brought their own uniqueness to the classroom and to collaborative teaching teams. They could tell you so much about what they have learned about kids and the teaching craft over the decades. I found that sharing a physical space with like-minded teachers was powerful and led to a daily sharing of ideas, of failures and successes, strategies, family stories, jokes, food, smiles, tears, theories, and frustrations. While there are great challenges in being a teacher, a school can be a truly great place to work.

Below is a letter given to me by one of my students, which I think is a good way to end my story. I feel like this letter goes deeper than a "thank you" and probably does a better job of representing what teaching is and what it can be than I could.

The letter is from a girl named Zeina. She wrote it when she learned that I would be retiring from public school teaching in the spring of 2024 (see Afterword for more on my retirement). She handwrote this letter to me and I've transcribed it here:

Dear Mr. Beckwith,

Anyone can be a teacher, but very few can be extraordinary. Before I ever met you, you had already changed the course of my life. I remember often coming home from school to hear about you and your class; a frequent conversation between me and my brother, Ali. He loved talking about your class, whether it was the latest story or the newest concept he learned. He started creating a simple text game in terminal, then it was opening 100 windows on the desktop, then it was GUI, and his projects continued to become more elaborate. I thought it was magic that he was able to do all that. I wanted to be able to do it, too, so I took basic coding classes in 8th grade, but it only made me dislike coding because the classes were boring and uninteractive.

Regardless, I wanted to meet you and take your classes because you made my brother so passionate about coding and I wanted to experience that, too. So I signed up.

From freshman year of high school until now, the only class I have ever strongly looked forward to is yours. You made coding feel simple yet powerful, interactive, and fun, and most of all, you inspired me to continue.

At first, I did find some ideas/concepts challenging, but with your guidance, it was much easier. You aren't only good at teaching, but also at handling/interacting with students. You've never once made me feel bad for making a mistake; you are encouraging and kind but not afraid to be honest. You have a way of making everyone feel safe around you. Maybe it's your sense of humor, your patience, or simply how you lead the class, but your class is the most comfortable I've ever been in. If I had the choice, I would have taken all the classes you teach.

I also love that you focus on creating a safe space for everyone by trying to increase diversity in computer science. On top of all that, you are extremely inspiring. I was hard set on being a teacher since I could speak, so any other career was not considered as an option to me, but after your classes, all I wanted do is code. I've never enjoyed anything as much as coding; I'm already planning out projects to do over the summer and I plan on majoring in computer science in college, thanks to you.

Without your classes, I never would make that choice, and although I can't speak for my brother, I'd like to think that you're part of the reason he's majoring in it, too.

You opened up that opportunity for many kids at CCHS who otherwise wouldn't have it, so even as you retire, your impact on the school will remain forever. You're inspiring and I hope to be like you someday. Although I've only known you for two years, I'll miss you. I hope you have an amazing retirement and thank you for being my teacher and everything else you've done. You're easily my favorite teacher I've ever had.

- Zeina

Me with my Coding Club students, 2017

AFTERWORD

By 2023, I had started to consider retiring early from teaching. I made a pros and cons list, a reasons-to-stay and reasons-to-go list. One of the most important items on the list was family. My father (that kid that was born in Mt. Auburn Hospital, that met my mother at a party and went on to become a scientist and social activist) had been diagnosed with Alzheimer's disease three years earlier. I was heavily involved in helping my mother and the family handle the whole situation and make big decisions about my father's health care. It was becoming difficult to do that while working full-time, twenty miles away. This wasn't the only reason, but it was an important one that led to my decision to retire from public school teaching at age sixty. I decided that the 2023-2024 school year would be my last. As of this writing, my father's condition has stabilized; he is doing well in a facility that is a half-mile walk from my mother's house where I grew up on Appleton Road and a mile and a half from our home in Arlington.

Can you guess what I did first, once I was retired? Two days after my official retirement date (my birthday), I got in my car and drove to the Woburn District Court to begin three months of grand jury duty—July to October—what fun! There are stories to tell from that experience, but we were barred from ever talking about the specifics of the more than 100 cases we heard during those three months, so instead I'll briefly describe something else I found myself doing shortly after the grand jury finished: my volunteer work at the *Cambridge Historical Commission* (CHC).

During the year that I was considering whether or not to retire, I had started to make a pretty extensive list of what I might do with myself if I decided to leave teaching, whenever that might be (sort of a "bucket list"). But in the first six or seven months after retiring, I was busy enough that I didn't even look at the list. Eventually, I dusted it off (well, *digitally* dusted it off) and took a look. One of the items on the list was to "*Find volunteer work,*" not that I really knew what that meant.

I had this list item in the back of my head in March of 2025 when I contacted the CHC, located next to City Hall in Cambridge. I had recently scanned some of my mother's old black and white photos she took in Harvard Square and wondered if some institution might like copies of them. I looked online and found the CHC. When I called them to ask if they were interested in the photos (they were), before hanging up I asked if they might have any volunteer opportunities—which they did. I came in and took a tour of the space. I found that the people, the projects they were working on, and the archives that they were processing were so interesting and impressive that I wanted to be a part of it.

Since the spring of 2025, I have been working to revamp their *Cambridge Women's Heritage Project* website and helping to increase the number of women who are profiled on that site. It is fulfilling and interesting work and I love working with the people there—and I love working on web projects and finding ways to make websites more interactive.

Another item on my checklist was "*Write my autobiography.*" I knew this one would be a huge amount of work, so I didn't want the weight of it to languish, to take up too much space in my head. I would take a stab at it and thought that it might take about a year to complete. In January of 2025, I dove in. Once I was on a roll, I was writing daily, whenever I had free time, almost obsessively. But I was really enjoying the process. It took from January to July to have a completed first draft.

I've learned a lot from "trying to be a writer." Like teaching, it's not what you think it is, at first. Surprisingly, though, I realized over time that writing a book does share a common theme with teaching, coding, and writing music. They are all creative and they all involve compromises and considering your audience. The process involved with each of them is helped by not blindly following the rules or the norms that you might have been told are important in that area. They can affect people's lives in a positive way. They're all complex and challenging—but so much fun! They all are helped by standing back, either in space or in time, and thinking carefully about what your goal is, what you've done so far, and making sure to look at what you're doing from a variety of perspectives.

I was recently writing this part of my story:

I only had one job offer at the time...

I came back a day later to pick up where I left off and that's when I realized that, *no, that doesn't sound right.* I tried it this way instead:

*I **had only** one job offer at the time...*

It sounded better! But why?

At first, I thought they each meant the exact same thing and they conveyed the same point, but the new one just *felt* better than the other. I biked over to my mother's house the next morning and, in passing, I mentioned the change to her (another benefit of retiring early is that I visit my mother most mornings, biking over for conversations about life, books, family history, politics, and anything else that comes up). All those years of teaching and practicing journalism kicked in and she explained to me that she agreed that I had chosen the better version, but also that the new one did indeed have a *different meaning* than the original one. We talked about why this was the case, having to do with the positioning of an adverb ("only") before or after the verb they modify ("to have"), but we also agreed that it wasn't that easy to describe the "why" in this case; we just knew it was different and it was clearer.

Does the order of those two words out of tens of thousands of words in this book matter very much? The jury's out on that one, but on that warm July morning, we both found ourselves engaged and immersed in the complexity of this simple question—and neither of us would have had it any other way.

* * * * *

IT WAS 1986, and I was at the end of my second year at UMass/Amherst. Back in Cambridge, a young woman named Sarah had a high school social studies paper due. For it, she needed to interview someone in her neighborhood about what they did for work. She ended up interviewing a neighbor from around the corner. The subject was my father, Jon Beckwith.

My mother, like me, saves everything. So it was no surprise to me when she produced a copy of this high school English paper from 38 years ago. In the paper, Sarah quotes my father's answer to her question of what his job as a scientist, a researcher, and a teacher was like. In a part of his answer, my father sums up much of what I've loved about the work I would do over the coming decades:

> *This job requires a lot of thinking, trying to think up new ideas and new ways of doing things. It also calls for figuring out your results when they're complicated. I enjoy the concepts, the thinking, and trying to be imaginative about things. This often involves talking with other people about things and coming up with ideas together.*

*****

In case you're wondering, Cori and I are doing well. Recently, we celebrated our 31st wedding anniversary. Our sons Daniel and Adam have each found interests that they are passionate about and they lead well-balanced lives. They care. And they love to laugh.

ACKNOWLEDGMENTS

This was fun. And challenging. And since I tend to be a very talkative person, while working on the book I talked over my feelings and my ideas and my approach with some people that I now want to thank and recognize for helping me through this work. They are the writer and friend Charles Coe, my mother Barbara Beckwith, my wife Cori Beckwith, and my friend Sara Kiesselbach.

* * * * *

Special thanks to Meta Partenheimer and Sara Kiesselbach for being gracious enough to read my manuscript when it "wasn't quite done" and being the first to give me a sense of whether this whole project had been worth it or not. It was!

I am grateful to friends and relatives whom I consulted for fact-checking and filling in details that may have slipped my mind. Those include Carol Stout, Barbara Beckwith, Cori Beckwith, Glenn Graf, Megan Frampton, and Gail Mazur.

* * * * *

Being a first-time author, it took me a while to realize that I had two major roles: first, I am the "story-teller," thinking through which parts of my life are interesting and relevant to the theme of the book; second, I am also the "writer," finding just the right combination of words to express my ideas and putting together the narrative in a way that would connect with the reader. The second part was more complex than I had thought. I cannot thank enough my mother, Barbara Beckwith, for volunteering to be my coach and writing mentor for this book. Hundreds of deleted words and rearranged sentences later, I came to fully appreciate the power of an editor who cares, who is patient, and who isn't held back by worrying about offending the writer. She helped make my sentences tighter and my memoir clearer. I am also grateful to Jan Gardner for combing through the final draft and applying her expert and meticulous copy editing to my manuscript.

*****

Special thanks to...

• My great-grandfather JB for making the voyage on that terrible ship in 1895, thereby making the Boston area my home—I've loved its uniqueness and continue to embrace it every day.

• My grandpa Joe for finding the strength to carry on when he lost his father at age 11.

• Both of my parents for being patient and modeling a life with meaning.

• All of my friends, family, colleagues, and band members, who have helped make life so very interesting for the last 60 years. In particular, there are close friends from when I was young that contributed to my developing perspective on life, but were not mentioned in the book: Rob Kirwan, Lawrence Price, Bobby Tynes, Paul Zacharia, Ann Jillian, Susannah Hopkins, Aime Degrenier, Ben Phillips, and Claire Taylor.

• John Yered and Marianne Gaffney who were great colleagues, supported my efforts at creating new courses, and helped make my long teaching career at CCHS a real blast!

*****

To friends who have passed on, Rest In Power: Eric Margid, Jimmy "Jem-I" Thompson, Prince Heron, Thomas Robert Anderson, John "Toto" Totovig, Patrick White, and Mike Crabtree

* * * * *

This flourish separator from vectorportal.com, creative commons:

ABOUT THE AUTHOR

Anthony Beckwith grew up and attended the public schools in Cambridge, Massachusetts. He received his B.S. in Mathematics from the University of Massachusetts at Amherst and a Master's in Education from the University of Massachusetts at Boston. Anthony retired after 30+ years of teaching high school mathematics and computer science.

His first teaching experiences were in the Boston public schools, but the majority of his career was spent at Concord-Carlisle High School in Concord, Massachusetts. He is an avid bicycler who loves to plan complex multi-day trips. He also produces original music and does volunteer work for a local historical society. Anthony is a huge fan of the show Seinfeld and the movie Groundhog Day and an even bigger fan of cats—any and all cats. He has created original web-based interactive tools for teachers and students and has maintained a detailed Boston Reggae history website for several years. Anthony lives with his wife and three angelic cats in Arlington, Massachusetts. They have two grown sons—one living in Somerville, Massachusetts; the other in Albuquerque, New Mexico.

For more on Anthony's web projects, reggae history page, original music, people stories, and more, visit **abeckwith.net**

FURTHER READING

A list of some my favorite books. Some have inspired me in my life and others have informed my writing of this memoir:

Biographies, Autobiographies and Memoirs:

This Life, Sidney Poitier
Harriet Jacobs: A Life, Jean Fagin Yellin
August Wilson: A Life, Patti Harnigan
Genius of Place: The Life of Frederick Law Olmsted, Justin Martin
Never Look an American in the Eye, Okey Ndibe
Finding Me: A Memoir, Viola Davis
David Suzuki: The Autobiography, David Suzuki
Ben Franklin: An American Life, Walter Isaacson
Catch a Fire: the Life of Bob Marley, Timothy White
Isaac Newton, James Gleick
Mala's Cat, Mala Kacenberg
The Autobiography of Malcolm X, Alex Haley
All About Me: My Remarkable Life in Show Business, Mel Brooks
Source Code, Bill Gates
Steve Jobs, Walter Isaacson
Into the Wild, John Krakauer
A Beautiful Mind, Sylvia Nassar
All Souls: A Family Story from Southie, Michael Patrick Mcdonald
Between the World and Me, Ta-Nehisi Coates
Never Caught: the Story of Ona Judge, Erica Armstrong Dunbar
To Tell the Truth Freely: The Life of Ida B. Wells, Mia Bay
Black Like Me, John Howard Griffin
Invisible Man, Ralph Ellison
Soul On Ice, Eldridge Cleaver

Bicycles & Bicycling:

The Long Ride, Lloyd Sumner
Odysseus' Last Stand: The Chronicles Of A Bicycle Nomad, Dave Stamboulis
Miles from Nowhere: A Round-the-world Bicycle Adventure, Barbara Savage
Life is a Wheel: A Passage Across America by Bicycle, Bruce Weber
It's All About the Bike: The Pursuit of Happiness on Two Wheels, Rob Penn
Two Wheels Good: The History and Mystery of the Bicycle, Judy Rosen
Jupiter's Travels, Ted Simon (travels on a *motor*cycle around the world)

About Comics:

Marvel Comics: The Untold Story, Sean Howe
Will Eisner: a Comics Biography, Steve Weiner and Dan Mazur
Marvel, Five Fabulous Decades of the World's Greatest Comics, Les Daniels
A Smithsonian Book of Comic-Book Comics, Bill Blackbeard, Martin Williams

Reggae:

Reggae International, Stephen David and Peter Simon
One Love: Life with Bob Marley and the Wailers, Lee Jaffe
Reggae Bloodlines: In Search of the Music and Culture of Jamaica, Stephen Davis and Peter Simon
Bass Culture: When Reggae Was King, Lloyd Bradley
Solid Foundation: An Oral History of Reggae, David Katz
The Rastafarians, Leonard Barrett
Wailing Blues: The Story of Bob Marley's Wailers, John Masouri

Local History:

Elsa's House Book, Elsa Dorfman
Harvard Square: an Illustrated History, Mo Lotman
Harvard Square: A Love Story, Catherine J. Turco
A History of Boston in 50 Objects, Joseph Bagley
The Death of an American Jewish Community, Hillel Levine
A City So Grand: The Rise of an American Metropolis, Boston 1850-1900, Stephen Puleo
The Other Boston Busing Story: What's Won and Lost Across the Boundary Line, Susan E. Eaton
The Hub: Boston Past and Present, Thomas H. O'Connor
The Boston Irish: A Political History, Thomas H. O'Connor
Common Ground: A Turbulent Decade in the Lives of Three American Families, J.Anthony Lukas
Boston Boy: Growing Up with Jazz and Other Rebellious Passions, Nat Hentoff
Eden on the Charles: The Making of Boston, Michael Rawson
Death at an Early Age: The Destruction of the Hearts and Minds of Negro Children in the Boston Public Schools, Jonathan Kozol

Sociology:

Race: How Blacks and Whites Think and Feel about the American Obsession, Studs Terkel
Working: People Talk About What They Do All Day and How They Feel About What They Do, Studs Terkel

Health:

Food First: Beyond the Myth of Scarcity, Frances Moore Lappe
Diet for a Small Planet, Frances Moore Lappe

The Food Revolution: How Your Diet Can Save Your Life and Our World, John Robbins

Spirituality:

Zen Mind, Beginner's Mind, Shunryu Suzuki
Tao Te Ching, Lao Tsu (Gia-Fu Fen and Jane English translation)
The Upanishads, Eknath Easwaran
Being Peace, Thich Nhat Hahn
Dharma Punx: A Memoir, Noah Levine

Mathematics & Computer Science:

The Mathematical Experience, Philip Davis & Ruben Hersh
Fermat's Enigma: The Epic Quest to Solve the World's Greatest Mathematical Problem, Simon Singh
The Innovators: How a Group of Hackers, Geniuses, and Geeks Created the Digital Revolution, Walter Isaacson
Technically Wrong: Sexist Apps, Biased Algorithms, and Other Threats of Toxic Tech, Sara Wachter-Boettcher
Nine Algorithms That Changed the Future: The Ingenious Ideas That Drive Today's Computers, John MacCormick
How Computers Work, Ron White
Algorithms to Live By: The Computer Science of Human Decisions, Brian Christian

Alzheimer's:

Ten Thousand Joys and Sorrows: A Couple's Journey Through Alzheimer's, Olivia Ames Hoblitzelle
Voices of Alzheimer's: Courage, Humor, Hope, and Love in the Face of Dementia, Betsy Peterson
Losing My Mind: An Intimate Look at Life with Alzheimer's, Thomas Debaggio
Remember: The Science of Memory and the Art of Forgetting, Lisa Genova
The Theft of Memory: Losing My Father, One Day at a Time, Jonathan Kozol

Writing:

On Writing: A Memoir of the Craft, Stephen King

www.ingramcontent.com/pod-product-compliance
Lightning Source LLC
Chambersburg PA
CBHW051822040426
42447CB00006B/327

* 9 7 9 8 9 9 3 1 0 8 7 0 4 *